— PRAISE FOR FLANN O'BRIEN —

"A real writer, with the true comic spirit."—James Joyce

"A lot of American readers think that S. J. Perelman was the humorous essayist of the century; but who did Perelman himself consider the best comic writer around? Flann O'Brien, aka Myles na Gopaleen, aka Brian O'Nolan."—*Washington Post Book World*

"A strange, original comic genius."—*New York Times*

"As with Scott Fitzgerald, there is a brilliant ease in his prose, a poignant grace glimmering off every page."—John Updike

"There is no doubt about it: O'Brien was a spectacularly gifted comic writer with a rich and very Irish endowment for sheer, glorious language. . . . And he had the other Irish gifts—of boisterous comic invention, and of raising a long glass in order to tell a daring tale."—*Newsweek*

"A man of black moods and (like Swift) of many ranks, Flann O'Brien brought the Irish tradition of verbal comedy to one of its perfections."
—Hugh Kenner

"If we don't cherish the work of Flann O'Brien we are stupid fools who don't deserve to have great men. Flann O'Brien is a very great man."
—Anthony Burgess

BOOKS BY FLANN O'BRIEN

— Novels —

At Swim-Two-Birds
The Third Policeman
The Poor Mouth (An Béal Bocht)
The Hard Life
The Dalkey Archive

— Collections —

The Best of Myles
Stories and Plays
A Flann O'Brien Reader
The Hair of the Dogma
Further Cuttings from Cruiskeen Lawn
Myles Away from Dublin
Myles Before Myles

Flann O'Brien

FURTHER CUTTINGS

FROM CRUISKEEN LAWN

Edited with a Preface by Kevin O'Nolan

Dalkey Archive Press

Originally published in Great Britain by Hart-Davis, MacGibbon Ltd., 1976
Copyright © 1976 by Evelyn O'Nolan
First U.S. edition, 2000

Library of Congress Cataloging-in-Publication Data:

O'Brien, Flann, 1911-1966.
       Further cuttings / Flann O'Brien. — 1st Dalkey Archive ed.
            p. cm.
       Selections from "Cruiskeen Lawn", O'Brien's regular column in the Irish times
        between 1947 and 1957.
       ISBN 1-56478-241-7 (alk. paper)
       1. Ireland—Literary collections. I. Title.

PR6029.N56 F87 2000
824'.912—dc21   00-020973

Partially funded by grants from the Lannan Foundation, the National Endowment for the
Arts, a federal agency, and the Illinois Arts Council, a state agency.

Dalkey Archive Press
www.dalkeyarchive.com

Printed on permanent/durable acid-free paper and bound in the United States of America.

Contents

Preface	9
The First Article	13
Monologues and Dialogues	16
The District and Other Courts	50
Bores	66
Latin Corner	73
Requiem Writings	80
Criticism	83
Politics	130
Controversy, Debate	153
Two Stories	186

Preface

This second volume of selections from 'Cruiskeen Lawn', Myles na Gopaleen's column in *The Irish Times*, covers, as does its companion, *The Hair of the Dogma*, roughly the period from 1947 to 1957, though some earlier and later pieces are included. As in *The Best of Myles*, some attempt has been made to classify pieces under various heads for the convenience of readers. Through half its history the column appeared under the name 'Cruiskeen Lawn' ('Full Jug'), without further clue as to what readers were actually having on any particular day.

It was thought worthwhile to reproduce in this volume, as a matter of interest, the first column of 'Cruiskeen Lawn', which was published on 4 October 1940. It appeared on the leader page of *The Irish Times*. Characteristically it was an attack on a leading article which had appeared in *The Irish Times* of 28 September. The article, under 'Cruiskeen Lawn', was headed 'From a Correspondent', and was subscribed 'An Broc' (i.e. The Badger). Before the next appearance of the column, on 12 October, the author had hit upon his final and most lasting pseudonym, Myles na Gopaleen.

In the succeeding weeks the frequent appearance of the column, mostly in Irish, led readers to wonder what had got into *The Irish Times*—something not quite healthy, to judge by some of the hostile letters which readers began to send in. But letters of approval began to appear too. In a short time the column was an accepted feature of the leader page.

This was its home for a long time. The author, from his sanctuary, often hurled abuse and criticism at his editor, R. M. Smyllie, across the thin line which divided his territory from the editorial column. Even as late as July 1951 he was writing:

Not the least of my duties is keeping an eye on the Editor of this newspaper and rebutting, for the benefit of our simpler readers, the various heresies propounded in his leading articles. Saturday's article was a great shock to me.

Alec Newman, who later became editor, was at that time

writing 'Irishman's Diary' under the pseudonym Quidnunc. He considered it unseemly that 'Cruiskeen Lawn' should appear on the editorial page and strenuously objected. But such objections fell on deaf ears. Later the column was moved to a safe distance on another page.

KEVIN O'NOLAN

The First Article

From a Correspondent

The other day a writer on the leader page of *The Irish Times* referred to the revival of the Irish language, not, indeed, for the first or last time in our rough island story. He said:

Surely the Government has realised by this time that it is very far from an easy task to eliminate and extend the use of the Irish language [*sic*] in place of English. The task would be hard enough in normal years, unless conversations could be limited to requests for food or drink and other expressions of the elementary wants of life, but at such a time as the present, when children all over the world are trying to keep pace with an influx of new words as a result of the war news bulletins, it becomes well-nigh impossible. Parents who confine the family meal-time discussions to conversations in Irish must find it very difficult to explain such words as air-raid warden, incendiary bomb, non-aggression pact, decontamination, and Molotoff bread-basket. Has Gaelic ingenuity, for that matter, stretched so far as to provide a really expressive and indigenous equivalent for the well-known 'Axis'?

One can imagine the stormy philological breakfasts that obtain in the households of the Gael:[1]

MOTHER: Anois, a Sheáin, caith do chuid bracháin.

SHAWN BEG (*peering into* The Irish Times): Ní maith liom brachán agus ní réidhtigheann sé le mo ghoile. Cuir Gaeidhilg ar '*Molotoff bread-basket*' le do thoil.

MOTHER: Anois, a Sheáin, bí suaimhneach agus caith do bhreicfeasta. Ní fhásfaidh tú aníos gan brachán agus bainne.

SHAWN BEG: Ní dóigh liom go bhfuil aon Ghaeidhilg ar '*Molotoff bread-basket*'. Ní'l sa Ghaeidhilg seo acht sean chanamhain ghagach. Cad chuige nach dtig linn Béarla a labhairt sa teach seo?

MOTHER: Mura mbíonn tú 'do thost ní bhfuighidh tú do phighin Dia Sathairn. Caith do brachán!

SHAWN BEG: *But, Maw! What's Molotoff bread-basket?*

MOTHER: BI DO THOST, ADEIRIM!

SHAWN BEG: Aw Maw, maith go leor. Ní chaithfead brachán go deo agus ní bheith aon mheas agam feasta ar Ghaedhlaibh.

MOTHER (*leading with her right*): Bhéarfad-sa *Molotoff bread-basket* duit, a thaisce, a aingilín bhig léigheanta.

Of course, there is no necessity for such scenes, because the Irish for Molotoff bread-basket is easy. One can say it several ways—[2]

> *Clíabh aráin an duine-uasail Ui Mhuilitíbh*
> *Manna Rúiseach*
> *Rúiskeen Lawn*
> *Feirín ó Stailín*
> *Brad-bhascaod Mhalatábh.*

The task of reviving Irish, we are told, would be hard 'unless conversations could be limited to requests for food and drink'. And who wants conversations on any other subject? Why not admit that hardly anybody ever thinks of anything else? If on and after tomorrow the entire *Irish Times* should be printed in Irish, there would not be a word about anything but food and drink. Those who find that they cannot do without 'incendiary bombs', 'decontamination', and the like, would have to get some other paper to accompany their ghoul's breakfast. The Irish would be full of *cainnt no ndaoine*, excerpts from *Séadna, corra-cainnte, sean-fhocla* and *dánta díreacha*, and would embody examples of *béarla féinne* and even *én-bhéarla* or bird dialect.

Finally, let it be said that the Irish for 'Axis' is '*Mol*', which sounds like short for Molotoff.

Mol an OGPU agus tiocfaidh siad.[3]

AN BROC

EDITOR'S NOTES:

1 In the dialogue the mother uses pleas and threats to get her son to eat his porridge. The son refuses and counters with a demand to know the Irish for Molotoff bread-basket, if indeed Irish can cope with such terms. Finally the mother gives him a box: 'I'll give you a Molotoff bread-basket, my precious, my little learned angel.'

2 The Irish words coined to translate 'Molotoff bread-
basket' range from translation, through 'Russian manna',
'Rúiskeen Lawn', a pun on Russia and Cruiskeen Lawn,
and 'a little gift from Stalin', to a comic transliteration of
the English term.

3 Finally '*Mol an UGPU*' etc. is a parody on an Irish proverb, '*Mol an Óige*' etc.: 'Praise the young and they will
advance.'

Monologues and Dialogues

Well I don't know. You often hear people complaining. I must say myself that I always got a great kick out of life.

I see?

You'll hear all sorts of complaints. 'I haven't enough money' or 'Me wife's sick for two year' or 'Th' income tax is goin' up' and so on and so forth. Sure man alive it's half the fun of the thing. I don't care what annyone says, I enjoy life. I get a great kick out of it.

That is very satisfactory.

Where would we all be, I'd like to know, if it was plain sailing all the time? No worry, no trouble, plenty of money, away down the country all the year round with your golf and your race meetin's and your game of cards. I'll tell you a damn funny thing about that.

What's funny?

You'd get fed up with it in no time. Ever heard of a happy millionaire?

I have.

They're the most bored crowd out and the half of them haven't got their health. A burden to themselves and to everybody else, hangin' around all day with time on their hands, not a worry in the world, dressed in the mornin' be flunkeys and all the rest of it. What good does it do them? Begob that crowd isn't long findin' out that money isn't everything. I seen plenty of them in Baldoyle in me time and a seedier-lookin' crowd you wouldn't find inside in the Dublin Union. A face on them as long as today and tomorrow. Misers that wouldn't throw a bone to a dog. Begob if that's what money does you're welcome to it.

Most wealthy people I know are happy, healthy and generous.

Take me own case. You have a fair idea of the way I'm fixed. You know I lost a child four years ago. I've had me ups and downs. In nineteen and twenty-two, when I was six months married I lost me job on the railways. Me sole crime was that I was an Irishman. And bedamn it but I enjoyed it all!

You appear to be an inverted sybarite?

And I'll tell you why. I take life as it comes. Do you folly me? I don't worry. I'll tell you what life is.

What?

Life is a game. The rules is there and the best man wins. I'll be forty-nine next February, and I can honestly say that I enjoyed every minute of it. I have no regrets and if I had me time again I believe I'd do the very same. In nineteen and twenty-nine I was arrested in Twickenham when the rugby was on. Do you mean to tell me I'm ashamed of that?

I don't mean to tell you anything.

Because I'm certainly not a bit ashamed of it. I was fined a quid. What's a quid?

Twenty shillings.

I seen quids spent more foolishly than that. It's part of the game. I got a rare kick out of the Twickenham business. And I can still take me bottle of stout with the next. It's all part of the game. Mean to tell me that it didn't make a better man of me?

I do not so mean.

Lookin' back over me lifetime I don't see annything I'd change. And there isn't another man alive that got more fun out of life. I had some of the fat and God knows you know yourself that I had me share of the lean. And I never weakened. I never complained nor wouldn't. I'll tell you what life is—it's a sort of a party. If you get the right angle to life you'll get great enjoyment out of it. Every day that passes I get a greater kick out of life. Handle it the wrong way and you're miserable. And I'll tell you a thing that never done annyone anny harm. Work.

Indeed? I was once in a mental home as a result of doing too much work.

Give me a job of work and I'm as happy as Larrie. I seen myself workin' for eighteen hours a day for two year and do you know what it is?

I do. You got a great kick out of it.

I was a happier man nor Henry Ford with all his money, I

enjoy life and I don't care who knows it. I get a great kick
out of it. And will till I die. You're not away? Well ...
cheers!

Hello begor!
Hello.
Haven't seen YOU for ages. How's thrix?
They are well.
Have you any books at all, there, at home?
I have.
I'll tell you a good wan. Did you ever come across a place
be the name of Lanx?
I did not.
Well do you know what's in Lanx?
No.
I'll tell you what's in Lanx—a sairten city be the name of
Liverpool. And in that sairten city there's a sairten big hos-
pital. Guess who's inside in the hospital? You'll never guess
—I'll tell you. The brother!
What happened your brother?
He come a clatter off a thramcar.
I see.
With the result is he's in the hospital stixled in bed readin'
away at the books. The ankle is gone, that man took a sore
fall for himself. I have a letter here he wrote me. He's for
takin'—wait now—he's for takin' LEGAL PROCEEDIN'S. He
does have a special solicitor sittin' be the bedside chattin' him
ten o'clock every mornin'. After that back to the books. He's
a divil for the books, the brother. Of course it's not supposed
to be known he's across the other side. He was over there
advisin'.
Advising whom?
Who do you think? Did you not hear about the war at all?
I did.
He's sendin' across now for more books. He has the place
across read out. Did you ever read a book be the name of *The
Phantom's Revenge?*
I did not.
Well the brother read it and do you know what he says
about it in this letter? AN ENGROSSING STUDY OF MANKIND

AT HANDIGRIPS WITH FATE. There's a book for you now. I'm surprised you never read that, you with the head on you. Do you never open a book at all?

Rarely.

Well here's another wan. Ever read *The Curtain of Love* be a man be the name of Lascelles de Groot?

Never. What is your relative's assessment of that?

Listen. A BOOK, says he, A BOOK THAT IS FIT TO TAKE ITS PLACE BESIDE THE IMMORTAL *DECAMERON* OF ... OF ...

Boccaccio?

That's the man. The brother takes a very high view of another book, a thing be the name of *An Offering of Swans*. What do you think he says? HERE ONE FINDS LINES, says he, NOT UNWORTHY OF THE SWAN OF AVON. What's that about now? What does he mean 'lines'?

He probably means 'lions'.

I see. Ever read a story called *Clara's Secret*?

No.

The brother takes a poor view. MERETRICIOUS PERFORM-ANCE, EMANATING AS IT DOES FROM A PERSON OF DOUBTFUL MORALS AND ATROCIOUS TASTE. He comes out very strong *there*, eh. Bedad that must be a terrible book? You haven't got it at home, I suppose?

I have not.

I see. The last one he has is called *Wagner: Madman or Genius?* The brother says *that* book—WHILE IT NEVER WILL REPLACE, IT WILL SUPPLEMENT THE STANDARD WORKS ON THE SUBJECT. Books about madmen begob—that's the latest. I'll have to see about gettin' some real mad books for the brother. Gob here's me bus! Cheers!

Bye-bye!

VISITOR: I pick up Auden.

DUBLIN MAN: Pairdin?

I pick up Auden. Jew now wear I get a 17 bus?

Pairdin?

Jew now wear the 17 bus stops I mean?

I beg yer pairdin?

I want to get to Witehall. Jew now wear Witehall is I mean?

Sairtintly I do. Do you know Westminister?

I pick up Auden?

You'll see the Houses of Parliamint there. You don't go across the river but you turn sharp left.

Wot you mean?

Pairdin?

Wot I wanted to know is wear do I get a 17 bus I mean.

A 17 bus? Shure yer croobs is on the very spot.

I pick up Auden?

Pairdin?

Wot I want to now is——

Gob here's a 17! If it's Drumcondra or Collins's Avenue or Whitehall you're goin' to, this is your man.

I say, I mean——

O.K. Cheers now!

(*Departs to Whitehall in a 17 bus, pleased that he has shown courtesy to a stranger. Visitor in desperation walks away from bus stop and stops another man, who happens to be a northern visitor.*)

I say, I pick up Auden . . .

Hullo there!

Aoh . . . Helloah, I mean . . .

At's a graun day the day.

Pod in? Jew now wear the buses stop I mean to say?

What was that?

Witehall. I want to get to Witehall.

Wheighthaul? At's a brave dastance to thon place.

Pod in?

What's that? Eye don't know what yer sayin'.

I say, jew now wear the 17 bus stops?

Over yonder.

Aoh. I've just been there I mean.

Eih?

Aaaah—jew now, I mean, witch way they gaoh?

Eye'm talon ye eye don't know what yer sayin'.

The 17 bus gaows to Witehall. Right?

Shur it's wratten up on thim.

Right! Now—witch way is the way to Witehall?

The mon in the bus'll know that, d'ye see.

But, re-ally, I mean. Aoh, wot's the good . . . !

Eye'm not shure meself. Wetilwesee! We'll ask this man.
(*Another Dublin man is stopped.*)

There's a mon here wants to go away to Wheighthaul, d'ye
awndherstawnd?

Pairdin?

I pick up Auden . . .

There's a stop forninst ye there awnd it's a question of
which way.

I beg yer pairdin?

Wot I want to knaow is how to get a bus. Wear to get eet I
mean to say.

Thus gentlemon is wantin' to know the way to Wheighthaul awnd eye'm a stranger, d'ye see.

Pairdin? Did ye say Whitehall?

Yes, Witehall.

Pairdin.

I *said* Witehall. Wear do I get a bus?

There's a stop a little bit down there. Where are goin'?

Wot? To the bus stop.

But shure me dear man look at here. Nobody but a madman would queue there.

Wot you mean?

Pairdin.

Wot you talking about?

The buses is all full there. I'll tell you your best man.

Pod in?

Your best man is to go above to Grafton Street. The crowd
from across do get off there.

Jew now wot I think of the Irish? I say—helloah! *TEXI!*
(*Rushes into road to hail passing taxi. Fails to see approach-
ing Whitehall bus, which kills him.*)

I was talking there the other day to a certain cool customer, a
party that I know and that you know, no names but you will
guess that I'm referring to a certain hop-off-my-thumb from
the County Meath, never done a day's work in his life, living
on the fat of the land and sponging on th' unfortunate sister
that got the insurance money the time she was near killed be
the car above at Blanchardstown. Do you know your man's
trouble? He's a bit short of *capital* if you don't mind! Know

what the poor man's complaining about? He has th'eight hundred all right—but where is he going to get th' other two hundred to make it the thousand? Can you beat it? Well begob I felt like leading him into the nearest and giving him a glass of malt for himself to cheer him up—or maybe he'd fancy a little tincture of brandy? Served up with dry ginger and a dart of th'angostura! Well bedad now, there's no limit in this world to the cheek of some people, I never seen anything to beat it and I was in and out of London many's a time. How much do you think *I* started off with at the game. *I'll* tell you how much—*five golden sovereigns in the heel of me fist no penny more or less.* I took a little place there near Sherrard Street and begob I'll never forget the oul wan of a landlady that I had to hand out a good-looking thirty bob rent in advance to before she'd as much as let me set foot in the place. Thirty good-looking shillings and I gave a pound to the mother on the Friday—*Monday morning I started in to work there with two pounds and ten shillings me only possessions in this mortal world!* Mind you in those days it was morning noon and night for me at the bench and I was a good five year at it before I had as much as a couple of bob to bring meself to the pictures with—every red penny went straight back into the business. I took on two lads in the first year, three more the year following and you can see for yourself what I have on me hands now. But I won't tell you anything only the absolute God's own truth every penny of it was earned and earned hard I was personally on the job there myself till about nine year ago. There's the whole twenty-one children reared and had a decent education there's four of them there on the floor before you now and I may tell you this and you may take it from me that there's very little change left out of two thousand pounds a year again you've paid the school fees, the piana fees, the French, the dancing, and, of course, the fencing classes. Ah no, don't let any wan tell you it's easy earned because do you know what I'm going to tell you and I'm seventy-five year at it this very week I'm going to tell you that it's not, no nor never was. There were times there—begob I laugh when I think of them now— there were times there when I'd come to the Mammy of a Saherda night, hand her the thirty bob and say Now Mammy, make the best you can of that till next week—maybe I'll have a few bob more on Friday! When the second was born, you'll laugh when you hear this, do you know how the doctor was paid? Oh, not a red fluke did the good man get, not a bob, but I asked would he accept a present of the half-moon job I had in mahogany with the usual veneers on it and I see the same table at the auction the day his stuff was sold when he died, a fifteen-pound note wouldn't buy it today.

Ah no, it's not easy earned. Don't let any wan tell you it's easy earned. And tell me this, what's the value of money today? Ah no, times is very changed—when I was a younger man you put a tanner in your pocket, up to th'Empire Theatre drinking pints above in the gods and then downtown again with a penny change to play with. Do you know what you could do with that penny? You could either ride five miles home on the top of an open thram—or buy yourself a dozen of Puck matches! No, don't believe it. It's not easy earned!

WIFE: This is Saturday.
HUSBAND: Yes.

You know who's coming on Christmas Day?

I do.

I'm going across to Charley's this evening, as I said. What are you going to do with yourself?

Oh, I don't know. Nothing in particular. Might go for a stroll later on.

A *stroll*?

Or read a book or something and go to bed early. That reminds me. There's a picture I want to see.

What picture?

I can never remember the names of pictures. You know that well.

Where's it on? Is it downtown?

Of course it's downtown.

When's this job in the bathroom supposed to start?

I'm still searching the town for turpentine. You can't use that paint without reducing it.

Couldn't you bring it back and get some other sort of paint?

Not today, anyway—they close early on Saturdays.

They're open late on this Saturday.

They're not. Hardware people don't sell Christmas stuff. Nobody buys a grate as a present.

They sell lamp-shades and youngsters' carpentry sets.

Of course, I could take a stroll down and see are they open. They might be, as you say. That crowd do a big trade.

I suppose there's no point in having wet paint about the place at Christmas. Since you're so long about it, another week or so won't make any difference. What book did you say you're going to read?

Book?

Book. You said you were going to sit in and read a book.

I haven't read a book for years.

What's wrong with your lighter?

It won't light.

Why don't you put petrol in it?

I spilt all the petrol last night. The bottle slipped.

When was this?

Oh, when I came home.

I see. Couldn't petrol be used instead of turpentine for paint?

I don't think so.

Stop clicking that thing. Here, take a match. What's your programme for Monday? Are you going into the office?

No damn fear, keep out of town is *my* motto.

You went in last year.

I *had* to last year. This year I've fixed things better. This year I'm staying put.

Then you'll be at home for lunch on Monday? Is that definite?

I probably won't have any lunch.

Why not?

Late breakfast, I want a good rest.

Again? You weren't up till nearly two today.

Another rest won't kill me.

Well, suppose you're up at two on Monday. What's your programme then?

Oh, just mess about. Later on I might take a stroll up to the golf club.

The *GOLF CLUB?*
Well—why not? I've a game more or less fixed up.
I hope you're not trying to be funny.
Fresh air and exercise never killed anyone.
Who said it did?
Nobody.
Well, I'm away. Ring me up about nine—I might want
something. And please see about that bulb in the hall.
I will. Goodbye for the present.
You're not coming with me?
I don't think so. I'll see that crowd time enough.
You know who's coming on Christmas Day?
I do.
You remember what happened last year?
I do.
So do I. Goodbye.

I do not suppose that there are many people in the world (of
all places) who, being persons accustomed to frequent places
of public resort, have not been subjected to the interesting
humiliation of being made party to what I choose to call a
monologous 'conversation'. Let the scene be pub, hotel
lounge or waiting room, it is all the same: it is terrible. You
are there. You are no eavesdropper, no Paul Pry. Yet if you
get up to go, it proves you are just all that.

Let me explain.

Let us suppose—imagination running quite riot—that you
are in the snug of a public house. (No smirking, now!) You
are confronted by a senile, white-headed pint, and you are
reading the evening paper as well as minding your own
business. You are vaguely aware of the presence of another
character in a soiled raincoat doing roughly the same thing.
The phone rings.

Before the curate has time to enter, the other character
comes up out of his evening paper and roars:

'I'M NOT HERE!'

You see? That is the primary crisis of this mysterious
canon. The call must be for him. It is probably the wife. And
he is not here. You? You begin positively to glower at the
print of your newspaper. Your concentration, your exclu-

siveness, is ferocious. Yet not a syllable of what follows can escape you. You are about to have it.

The curate[1] arrives, takes off the receiver, listens intently for a period that seems a year, and then says:

'Yooze shpakin'?'

Another year passes. Dimly you can hear a lengthy reply like 'Zzzzzzzzzzzzzzzzzzzzzzzzzzzzzzzz'.

'Oi see,' the curate says. 'He was in earlier wait'll see is he here now he doesn't stay long he's not touchin' anthin' I undherstand.'

During this passage the character in the raincoat is so un-hearing and motionless that he appears to be dead. The curate, covering the instrument with the great red ham of his hand, in what is intended to be a 'whisper', says:

'It's one of the chiners, Mick.'

I will not try to describe the slow, majestic disengagement of this Mick from his chair. He takes the instrument from the curate without a word, and then your agony begins.

MICK: Hello.
INSTRUMENT: Zzzzzzzzzzzzzzzzzzzzzzzz.
What? Is it Jack?
Zzzzz.
Well do you know by gob I was thinking about you yester-day what am I talking about it was this morning when his nabs and the young wan with him down in Ussher's Island.
Zzzzzz. Zzzzzzzzzzzzzzzzzzzzz.
Indeed and I did. A Sahurda a Mrs Lawlor's a Naas. Brandy and ginger ale if you don't mind, and LARGE WANS. Do you know what it is, there's no living doubt.
ZZZZZZZZZZ.
Sairtintly.
Zzz. Zzzzzzzzzzzzzzzzzz. Zzzzz. Zzz.
Now listen here to me. Do you know what I'm going to tell you? That class of thing can't last. I seen the same crowd in a sairtin place in Newbridge a Easter Monda stuck inside in a back snug with four Free State Army privates, two super-visors out of the Turf Board supervisin' pints good-o, a

[1] See note on p. 28.

certain lassie that you know and that I know in the middle of them, and the whole crowd singin' Boolavogue. I'd boolavogue them if I had me way. I'll tell you that. How is it done? Where do all the readies come from? Where do they get it if they don't get it the wan way?

Zzzzzz. Zzzzzzzzzzzzzzzz. Zzzzz. Zzzzzzzzzz. Zzzzzzzzz. Zzz. ZZZ. Zzzzzzzzzzzzzzzzzzzz.

By gob you're right there.

Zzzzzzzzzzzzzzzzzzzzz.

WHO?

Zzzzzzzzzzzzzz.

Drum . . . con . . . dra? What?

Zzzzzzzz. Zzzzzzzzzzzzzzzzzzzzzz. Zzzzzzzzzzzz.

What? What hat?

Zzzzzzzz. Zzzzzzzzz. Zzz zzz zzz.

But sure listen here to me, me good man, that thing has bin goin' on all the time. That crowd has us all be the hasp, always had.

Zzzzz. Zzzzzzzzzzzzzzzzz?

Now listen. I never like to see that class of stuff mentioned in the papers at all. Supposin', now, your own sister was . . . Hah?

Zzzzzzzzzzz!

Matteradamn. It's not right. Doesn't do nobody any good at all. I hear the other chiners is leppin' over it.

Zzzzzzzz. Zzz. Zzzzzzzzzzzzzzzzzz.

Maby you're not far wrong there. I never heard of a means test in that particular quarter. By the gor I seen meself thinkin' that it might be no harm at all to have not wan but two houses and mothor cars to get me from the wan to th'other. All the same, Jack . . .

Zzzzzzzz!

Lave that alone now. How is the missus?

Zzzzzzzz!

Is that a fact? Well do you know what it is you are a terrible man.

ZZZZZZ. ZZZZZZ. Zzzzzzz.

But shure it's only nature me dear man . . .

Now supervenes the master-climax of the canon. The mysterious 'conversation' proceeds on even keel. Like this:

Zzzzzz. Zzzzzz.
You may bet your life on it.
Zzzz. Zzzzzzzz. Zzzzzzzzzzzzzz. Zzzzzz. Zzzzzzzzzzz.
Hello! (*Very urgently*) Hello! Is THAT JACK?
Let us leave him (or them) on that superb note. Only at the end of a long and intimate conversation does a doubt strike Mick that he has been conversing with a total stranger.

He does not realise, as I do, that it makes no difference. The 'conversation' would be quite the same, anyway.

I know them fellas.

NOTE: Curate, i.e. barman.

I've been on these cars now man and boy for the last seventy or eighty years and I'm telling you this much that the like of the carry-on that is to be seen nowadays is something shocking. Even out here now—supposed to be a good district and all that sort of thing—you see them there going wild like . . . like slum children for all the world. You talk about afther the last war I never seen anything like this. *Drinking, too! Yes!* Chislers there that high . . .! I brought a woman down from Kenilworth Square there the other night, a woman and her daughter she goes inside and the daughter is outside on the car and the mother inside pays for her. I go up and the next thing is I'm asked *for a match*! Have I got a match will I give her one? She begs my pardon? What was that? A bolder-looking article I haven't set two eyes on in me whole lifetime. Talk about paint . . . and the powder? I have a match of course but I said no and said it loud enough too—I wouldn't have that on me conscience—a child of ten if you don't mind! Of course I need hardly tell you she *got* a light off another man on the car . . . and there she was there puffing away fag after fag inhaling and all betther nor I could do it meself! Where do you suppose that sort of thing is going to end?

And the other thing of course they talk about England faith then island of saints and scholars how are you! I do often think . . . I do often think that the way things is shaping you'll see another war and do you know where it'll be fought this time? Here! Mark me words now. Believe me or believe

me not. It'll have to come, government and people and all'll
have to pay. And there's another thing. I'm a man that's not
a temperance advocate or anything like that. On the other
hand I'm not a heavy dhrinker what you might call but I'll
have an odd bottle of stout there with the next man. I was
never a man for the malt at all that's a thing you have to be
born to, but the thing that I can't make out is this—how do
these young girls, how in the name of heavens do they
manage to hold it?

I'm telling you that in this city it's not better but worse
things is getting. These lounge bars whatever you call them
might as well all be shut up. Any hour of the night or day you
go in there what do you find girls, young women, married
women and oul' wans all sitting there knocking back their
jars with the best of them. Ever since the war started of
course you have all the men across the other side and then
what happens only the wives is out dhrinking in them lounge
bars. And not be themselves either. Where is all that going to
end would you mind telling me?

I was outside there in a certain public house the other
night having a bottle of stout and there was a young girl and
a fellow beside me. I had the two bottles of stout and took me
lave, and will you believe me that in that time that girl had
four glasses of malt! And that's not all of it. The lad with her
was drinking the black stuff and in this pub you could only
get one half for each person. Do you know what he did each
time? One bottle of the black and two halves and when he
brings them back to the table both the halves is fitted into the
wan glass! There I was for one short half an hour and how
much was your man after spending in that short time? And
do you mane to tell me that he was doing that for nothing?
Aaaaahhh.

God be with the days when you never seen a respectable
girl in a public house is what I say—but this girl *was* respectable. Would that have happened in the old days? I'll tell
you this much the father and the mother and the two sisters
is all buried now, God be good to them, but up to the day
they died them two girls had to be in every night at ten
o'clock. Was there anything wrong with that? I think not and
I'll tell you wan thing, there was never heaard of anything

going wrong *there* you can take my word for that. I'm not a man meself that has anny children, but would any daughter of mine be going on with that class of carry-on in my life-time? Hah? I think not. In at ten o'clock every night and as simple as decent girls as the day is long. And what's wrong with that would you mind telling me?

This tireless reporter records today, for the benefit of readers as well as p-austerity, another conversation which he has had in a pub. It is remarkable for two facts—the writer did not know the other person, his name or station, and—though the writer participated in the conversation—he was at no time vouchsafed even a clue as to what the conversation was *about*.

Where do you lave that crowd now?

I do not know.

A right crowd.

Yes.

And your other men. Where do you lave THEM?

Exactly.

I seen all that crowd and knuwn them and they're no use to annybody.

I agree.

They're no use to me nor to you nor annybody anny-where. Do you folly me?

I think I do.

I never seen a greater crowd of hooks in me life so help me.

They are certainly bad.

I seen them all and I knuwn them all and they're no damn good.

I see.

I knuwn them? What am I talking about I seen meself sittin' down with their fathers in growlers going off to the Strawberry Beds of a Sunda on a pic-a-nic. Silk hats and no breakfast if you know what I mean.

I think I do.

I knuwn one of them fellas well. Ball-dancin' three times a week with a married wumman.

Is that a fact?

I need hardly remark that the married wumman wasn't the

wumman he was married to. Do you get me point? How are you for Catholic Ireland?

How are you indeed!

At wan time there was wan thing that put a stop to his gallup. Ball-dancing only wanst a week. Do you know why?

Shortage of money, I suppose.

MONEY? (*Steps back, examining me to see whether I have two heads.*) MONEY? What are you talking about sure that man went in nowhere bar on a free pass. Money? (*Laughs mirthlessly.*) I'll tell you why.

Why?

He used to borry a monkey-suit off a waiter in the Bailey.

I see.

With the result is he could go dancin' only on the waiter's half-day, a Thursda.

Understand it now.

In anny case he got to know four waiters out the old Clarence and at the heel of the hunt could put his hand on a monkey-suit anny day of the week. A home-wrecker, that's what that fella was. Two of the uncles finished up in the 'gorman.

I suppose drink was at the root of the trouble.

Drink? I asked one of that crowd one day in what is now Aherne's of Camden Street would he like a small wan. Didn't know what I was talking about at all. *A what?* says he. Speaking very clear, I asked him again would he have a SMALL WHISKEY. Sairtintly, says he, I'll have a ball of malt. That'll give you some idea. That crowd was no good to annybody. I knuwn them. I SEEN them.

There is no living doubt.

And their fathers was no good to annybody. I had a certain bit of business to do with wan of them on a particular day and I called to the house. A whole crowd of kids inside roarin' and the wife in bed too weak to stand up from starvation. A skillet of cabbage soup was been got ready be the eldest girl for the 'dinner'. This was shortly after Cosgrove set up the Free State.

That was some time ago.

And where do you think My Nabs was?

I cannot imagine.

In a certain particular place in Drumcondra that *I* know and that *you* know, stuck in the back snug with two Free State Army privates and a wumman of a certain class.

I see.

Drinking malt good-o, the four of them trying to sell somebody's else's house in Clyde Road to some mad hop-off-my-thumb from the County Carlow. Country Mug is invited to make a deposit of one hundred notes in the snug there and then as a guarantee of his good faith. And do you think the celebrations stopped when the pub closed?

I doubt it.

Not at all. All out doing the bonafide in a taxi that never got paid at the heel of the hunt.

Deplorable behaviour.

Another of that crowd come home with the milk wan morning in a monkey-suit to find the sticks of furniture in the gutter, lurried out be the Corporation because this fella that spent the night dancin' couldn't possibly afford the maganificent sum of WAN POUND TWO SHILLIN'S for rates. But there was a bed left in the house. Do you know why?

I certainly do not.

Because the bed was holding the brother, home in the jigs from the British Army, that couldn't be put out because he hadn't a trousers. Your man in the monkey-suit had them pawned on him.

Disgraceful.

That crowd is no use at all, and their fathers was no use.

I agree.

Mind that crowd.

I will. Bye-bye.

(Phew!)

I was below in the Bode Eega th'other night.

I see.

I seen two of them down there.

Lave me alone.

Scoffing malt, the pair of them.

Don't say another word to me at all.

And large ones at that!

(This is still another verbatim note of a conversation carefully

*overheard by the present writer in, more betoken his own place,
the Scotch House.)*
 Shure what are you talking about? Where are we?
 Lave it alone.
 You never said a truer word.
 Lave it alone.
 LARGE ones, hah?
 If I said it once I said it twenty times.
Nothing but large Irish whiskeys and nothing would do
them only soda in it if you plaze. And the poor out in the
frost digging turf out of Glencullen.
 Didn't I tell you?
 A right crowd if you like.
 Mind them fellows.
 That crowd has us all be the hair.
 A right crowd of chiners.
 Drinking LARGE ones if you don't mind?
 Don't be talking to me.
 Do you know what I mean?
 Lave it alone now like a good man.
 I seen a good few in me day. I seen them in the Catholic
and Commercial Club, hatchin' out plans to blow up the
Maple Hotel in Kildare Street.
 I knuwn that crowd meself.
 I seen all them cross-channel revolutionary lads—Pearse,
Griffith, Childers—I seen them interfering with the trams, a
right how-are-you for a man of my age coming out of the
Empire Theatre in Dame Street.
 And that's not today nor yesterday.
 The characters that makes trouble here is all English.
 Don't be talking to me. Did you ever hear of a Dubalin
man kicking up trouble?
 All of them crowd is either Englishmen or lads out of the
county of Kildare. Jockeys. The papers is full of them fellas.
Mind them lads. Watch them fellas. Ireland has produced
good men but when it comes to turning out scruff—do you
know what it is?—we give best to no country in the whole
world, injuns nor jewmen. *Now* do you understand me? Do
I make me point clear?
 Don't be talking man.

Do you folly me?

Where do you lave your other men? The insurance crowd?

Would you lave me alone for goodness sake.

Or the hire-purchase crowd—the home for happy brides but please send yer money to Great Throgmorton Street. Hah?

Would you lave me alone and don't be talkin'.

Hah?

I seen all that crowd and I knuwn them well. I seen them.

I seen them meself.

I knuwn that crowd well.

It's a crowd that's no use to any country.

I seen them meself.

And I knuwn them and knuwn them well.

I know them—I seen them.

I knuwn them well in the days gone by.

(*Exit of pained eavesdropper.*)

Accepting hospitality in other people's houses can sometimes be a hazardous undertaking. It is very dangerous, for instance, to call on other people without any warning, for you may be walking right into the epicentre of a first-class family row. It is really safer not to visit other people at all but to meet them only on the neutral battlefields provided by hotels. Did you ever upset a bottle of stout on your hostess's new carpet? Know what I mean?

Let me record an odd little adventure which befell me recently. I went down the country to visit some old friends— *by invitation*, let me add. A pleasant married couple, well set up.

The husband, a most affable man, was fond of good company and good talk—why else should he have asked me to come to his house?—and he was most *flahooluck*, in the accepted sense. As midnight approached I made the usual dishonest remarks about getting into a hotel. Under no circumstances, of course—a room had been got ready for me in the house. So there had, but it was three in the morning before I got to it.

It was ten o'clock when I awoke. One does not take liberties about lying late abed in other people's houses: that is another of the snags. Though very tired, I arose, performed a careful toilet and went downstairs. The lady of the house was in the dining room and greeted me brightly. Yes, it was a beautiful morning. What would I like for breakfast?

Sundry grunts and noises upstairs indicated that the host was astir. I heard him heavily pounding down the stairs just as his wife was handing me a glass of orange juice. He came into the room in a dressing gown.

Then it happened.

Having given me what appeared to be a nod, he turned to his wife and said:

'Alla poo anidee tie peat.'

Family double-talk, perhaps—but the thing disturbed me. I felt an intruder.

'I do not,' the wife said.

'Glauwacack ant sohomouse asassopa,' he said. 'Gowl a gurda.'

'You'd know yourself if you kept your wits about you,' the wife said.

'Gumpa slourish shaga peat, chacha peat,' he growled.

'Well, I suppose we'll have to,' she replied.

She had been sitting and stood up. A horrible fear clawed at my heart. *She was going to leave the room!*

'Gushka goms,' he said.

And she did leave the room, giving me a strange smile. I was alone with this man!

'Choora gushka goms peat,' he said to me—amiably, I thought.

I nodded and smiled. I hastily averted this smile, fearing it was too ghastly, and quickly foostered out a packet of cigarettes. He took one. The lighting of a cigarette gave me a few more seconds in which to do fast thinking.

'Carda fyung trealis koo foind cha kaka peat,' he observed. *Salvation!*

I heard the footsteps of the wife returning. She came into the room carrying *his* orange juice. He took the glass but did not drink. Instead he put his fingers in it and took out two rows of teeth which he deftly installed in his mouth.

'It really *is* a beautiful morning,' he said to me in perfect English. 'The very morning for a game of golf.'

What is that thing Spenser wrote some years ago——?

> Sleep after toyle, port after stormie seas,
> Ease after warre, death after life, does greatly please.

Something of the kind came into my head the other day in my own place (the Scotch House) when Foley and Purcell appeared at my private office looking for audience.

I was vastly amused.

The crowd immured in the Bank of Ireland (hereinafter known as 'the directors') got on the blower to the Scotch House, and made it known to my staff that nothing would do them only get two dozen 'snipes' of Guinness's stout for their lunch. I thought the order for 'snipes' as distinct from bottles was a fair estimate of the appetite of these persons for what we call life.

We sent our man up with the two dozen 'snipes'. The observers were there. Our man believes in trade unionism, and very properly so. At the same time he wasn't sure that these 'observers' constituted a legal picket. So he rang up his own union. The head buckcat in the union gave the inevitable reply that a 'dispute' was in progress. (Talk about understatement?) Our man—I have since formally knighted him—brought the twenty-four snipes back to the Scotch House.

I will now change the subject, recording for the information of posterity a conversation I overheard in the same Scotch House between two persons (unidentified) on a subject (wholly unidentified):

1: What do you think of them now?

2: I told you about that crowd.

1: NOW where are we?

2: I knuwn that crowd well. Watch them fellas.

1: I mean to say.

2: I said it before and I'll say it again. Watch them chiners. They has us be the hasp.

1: Do you know what I mean? Do you get me point? And where do you lave Maynooth?

2: Now listen here to me like a good man. Do you know what I'm going to tell you. That crowd has the whole lot of us destroyed. Do you know what I'm telling you? Shure we're not men at all nor half men. Do you know what we are?

1: I certainly do.

2: Of course you do. Don't say another word.

1: And come here to me. What about your other men? Now you're talking.

2: Don't say another word about it at all.

1: And what about your men across the water?

2: Would you lave me alone and not be talkin' to me at all.

1: There is no living doubt.

2: I knuwn some of that crowd when they hadn't a rag on their backs nor couldn't find the price of a pint between ten of them. I knuwn them well. I seen them. I know that crowd. I seen me unfortunate farther murdered by the same chiners. They forced money on the unfortunate man when he hadn't a tosser and the next thing the family knuwn was that the boss was cocked up in a castle in the County Wickala.

1: Shure don't I know all about it? *Give us two more, Mick, and put it on the slate!*

2: Do you get me point? Do you folly me?

1: I know what I'd do with that crowd if I had me way.

2: Do you folly me?

1: Do you know what it is? I seen that crowd and I know them. I knuwn all that gang years ago. I seen them and I know them all. Mind them fellas. Keep the weather-eye open for every man-jack of them. That's a crowd that's no use.

2: Do you know what I'm going to tell you . . .?

(*I went home at this stage. Too damn well I knew what he was going to tell his companion and me, i.e., that that crowd was no good at all under any circumstances. What on earth were they talking about in this unique clueless discussion almost totally devoted to telling each other to shut up? C.I.E.? G.N.R.? The pork butchers? Meself, itself?*

I dunno.

Does it matter, awfully, anyway?)

Is it YERSELF?

It is.

Well how are you at all, the brother is back above in the digs and we're all back, the bottom has fall out of that

London job. And I'll tell you a damn good wan. Sir Laurence
Olivier says that neither meself nor the brother will be anny
good as ballet dancers. Just because the pair of us is Roman
Catholics. All the crowd is home out of the London theatres
and studios.

No wonder.

The brother has the wind up the landlady above in the
digs.

Is that so?

The brother kicked up a terrible barney in the digs the
night he come home, after been charged twenty-four bar be
the customs at Kingstown for his dancin' pumps. What's
this, says the customs man? Them's me pumps, says the
brother. I'm a dancin' artist. Is that so, says the customs
man, you can pump out twenty-four bob like a flash or I'll
impound your pumps and get them pumped down be way of
the sewers to the Chief Collector of Customs and Excise
above in Dublin Castle and that will fix you, me bould
segotia, says the customs man. Furthermore, says he, have
you anny copies of *Lilliput* on you at all? But the brother was
ready for him. A great man the brother for the rep R tea.
'WHAT,' says he, 'LILLIPUT? I never seen that thing at all, I
understand it's run be the Glenavy family that's tryin to put
the G.N.R. on the backs of the taxpayers, I never had anny
time for that crowd.' Your man's face fell.

No wonder again.

Wait till you hear. The customs man has another shot in
the locker. What's this in the bottle, says he. That's bay rum
for me hair, says the brother—I'm losin' me hair. So am I,
says the customs man, wait till I have a look at this inside in
the office. He comes out after a few minits with the bottle half
empty and no wonder you're goin' bald, says he, who
wouldn't be if that's the treatment. The brother, cute as a
hawk, takes the half bottle back and changes the subject. I
thought, says he, that Drumcondra was in charge of this
country since I left. Do you know what's goin' on these
boats? The customs man couldn't answer immediately because he had swallied half of the brother's malt; he can't talk
right.

What did he say ultimately?

He made a class of a noise in his neck. You're a liar, says the brother, and you're a double-liar. I spent four hours, says he, lyin' in a lifeboat because there's no other place to lie in. *Really?*

Too true. When he come home the brother warneded the landlady about evil literature. Th'unfortunate woman had a copy of the Red Guide on th'hallstand. Is it true that you're putting a match to the whole town? That's what the crowd is sayin'.

Not true?

The brother says that you are a great man for Stravinsky's 'Fire Bug'. Is that a fact?

It is not a fact.

Did you put a match to th'Abbey?

I did not.

Of course, if you done it you wouldn't be the first to shout you done it. The brother says you're a very cagey piece of work.

I would need to be if I must live in the same world as your relative.

Miss Downes of the Cumberland Hotel in Westland Row says you put a match to the *Irish Times*. Tighe of the Moira says the same and so does Joe of Jury's, Gallagher of the Hibernian insurance crowd has the same story, Cavey has it out in Bray, Kenneth Reddin' was telling a crowd of oul wans covered with black frocks and beads the same story at a tea party last Sunday, and Inspector Mick Farrell is getting a file up on the subject. Do you know what the brother says?

I certainly do not.

The brother says there is no smoke without fire.

Is that so?

But I'll tell you what the brother said as well. YOUR MAN IS PAIRFECTLY RIGHT, says the brother. That crowd is no good says he, was never any good, says he, nor won't be any good. That crowd is no good at all to anybody and in any case is all mad. Your man, says the brother, is courageously performing a national duty without regard to pairsinal safety and even if he gets locked up itself, Sean Kavanagh above in the 'Joy will lend him the Penguins to have a good read for himself.

Thanks.

Why don't you put a match to the Dail Eireann?

Arson is not my profession.

I will tell you a good wan. There is going to be murder to-night. When he was across for the last six years, the dress suit was et be rats.

Most unfortunate.

Un . . . fort . . . unate? Is that all you have to say?

What more can I say?

By gob maybe you're a wise man to keep your mouth shut. Here's me bus. Cheers!

Cheers!

Ah but shure listen you don't know the half of it. Me dear man luckit here.

Who is the crowd that is up in Dubbalin today with the white coats and the black clawhammers and the knives and the forks and the sneers on their gobs at the likes of you and me handing out our good money to them and getting nothing but impudence in return—answer me that? O it's all damn fine. They have the ball at their feet now they have us where they want us we're nobody we're oney Shawn and Shaymus and it's 'I'm sorry me good man, I can do nothing for you' or 'Have you an appointment plaze?' But *I* remember the time when it was another story. Another story entirely. Yes. I remember a time begob when mattheradamn you had oney two and sixpence in the throuser pocket you got a fair deal, you were a blooming honest-to-God customer and it was all smiles and Yessir and Nosir and How is Mrs M. this weather I hope well? I seen that. I lived through all of that. I know what I'm talking about ask Jem here he'll tell you. I seen it all. And *now*—I . . . seen . . . the other act!!!! With me own two eyes, right here in Dubballinn a town I was born and reared in oney sometimes do you know what it is I'd as soon say it's from Injuh I am. At *least* in Injuh if you have the white coat on and you can write you're probably a dacent civil sairvint from Ailebury Road that knows his place and doesn't talk out of turn for the very good reason that he has a pet aversion from having his teeth smashed in be a clatther of a polo bat now d'ye see what I'm afther? (Mind you, that's a world that's dying out *too* and it was a damn fine world in its day divilabetther I remember the time you were no one if you hadn't at least six of the uncles in the Hong Kong Mounted Polis ask Jem here he'll tell you. And that day, I may tell you here and now, is gone for ever and a very good day it was when the sairvint knew his place and gev way to his betthers. It was all master and man in days and you may say what you like there was a . . . very . . . sthrong . . . bond of . . . genuine affection and loyalty between the two. All gone be the blooming board now nothing oney sit-down strikes, lock-outs, squatters and me bould Jem Larkin in the saddle again as large as life and twice as handsome!)

I'm an ordinary Dubballinn maaan me parents was all in this city when the crowd of whippersnappers that's going nowadays wasn't even thought of. I'm an honest man. *And* of course I'm a poor man. (I *won't* keep quiet I'm oney saying what's the blooming truth!) *I* can't afford to splash me money around the place like wather. And, as far as I can see, it's got to the stage here when *you have to have money*!!! Oooooh, there's a quare change come over things since the old days when no matter how poor a class of a pub you were in every third drink was on the house!!! Yiss!!! What are you laughing at ask Jem here he'll tell you. (I'm not shouting bring us three more halves Jack and a naggin for herself she's not well at all . . . that's a good lad.) Do you know what I seen here, *on this very spot*, oney the other night? Do you know a certain bettin' man that you know and that I know? Do you know the wife of that before-mentioned mhaaan with a back on her that all it needs is the number for you to take it for a hackanay cab? Well, I was . . . in . . . here, d'ye see? I dhropped in for a few cigarettes, you *know*, the head down going about me business quietly not minding annyone not looking for trouble wanted to get home for *wan* night in the week, d'ye know? Suddenly I feel the big hand on me back and me neck is scorched be the blast of hot malted air from the troat of this sairten mhaaan. *I* . . . *was* . . . *very* . . . *cool with him, of course.* You *know*? I have very little time for his type at the best of times. Goodnight, says I, I must be off now; and I make a dart for the door. Well . . . the next thing I know the coat is wrenched offa me back. I'm grabbed be the elbow, I'm lifted

back upon the stool and what have I in me hand oney . . . the usual, with a dash of peppermint! I was . . . very, very annoyed do you know what I mane? Well, annyway, in the heel of the hunt, to make a long story short, there I am. I'm talking to the Missis, ye *know*, but I see what's going on between the lad and the villyin in the white coat behind the baar. Here . . . I'll give it to you word for word you won't believe me. *Much is that?* Three and tenpence sir. *Three and ten, eh, hould on there till I see have I it.* Well it was as good as a play the lad took out what was in *wan* pocket medals, paper clips, fuses, sthring, butter scotch and all, and carefully counts out . . . wan two shillin' piece . . . wan shillin', a tanner . . . a thruppenny bit . . . and a bright new copper penny!!! Hah? *Wait till you hear!* He shoves the lot across the counter. *Is that right?* Yessir all correct. *Fair enough. Here's something for yourself.* He puts the hand into the inside jacket pocket, takes out the wallet . . . *and counts out a pound note to your man in the white coat! As . . . a . . .* TIP!!! Wait till you hear!! Thank you sir says your man and walks away. Well you can believe it or not I seen it with me own two eyes and you can ask Jem here I told him all about it too. But you know what it manes of course? It means that you and I are *nowhere*! You come in there for a bit of a feed before going to bed and if you was to go down on your bended knees it's the same thing you'll get the point steak you could sole your shoes with, the peas swimming in breadsoda, the cold mash with water, lumps and maggots—follied, I need hairdly say, be brown frozen varnish! (Coffee, if you don't mind!) *Nine and fourpence!* NINE AND FOURPENCE! That's Dubballinn for you, that's the city I seen a blaze of lights in the old days and poor Dudley riding up Dame Street on the white horse, you put a bob in your pocket and you have a feed at the counter in Corless's, you bring a mot to the Empire, have six pints in the bar, go home in a cab . . . *and have change*!!!!!
Shure luckit here don't be talking to me, man.

Scene, a bridge. Present is a noonday lounger in drunken dungarees. He leans. He has a strong fur face which appears to have been treated with tar and metal filings applied. His hands seem to be covered with bark. He is withered.

Is it two, I suppose?
I shouldn't think so—that was the one fifteen just now.
Wrrrrwtgfrlooaadddhmm . . .
Ibegyourpardon?
Hah? (*Shakes himself.*) Oh. Hmm. We're waiting for a cargo to come in, that's what it is. (*Sudden straightening, walks away from bridge, shouts.*) It's no good, no use at all, d'yeh see what I mean . . .
I don't quite . . .
This working for the railway, it's no kind of life . . . Do you see why, hah?
Do you feel there's no future in it?
Whaaaah? Oh, Yeh, that's it. (*Subsides, elbows on the coping again.*) It's waiting around like this, d'yeh see. Here you are, do you understand. (*Brings up the face face to face and the rain pouring past the two figures on to the track.*) You're . . . waiting around like this . . . and . . . at the same time . . . you've got to be as good as the next one. Now do you see?
Um . . . Yes.
That's the railway for you and I know them.
You feel that hours are too long and pay too small?
(*Reopens sharply the agonised eyes, shouts*) NOT AT ALL, OF COURSE NOT THE PAY IS ALL RIGHT . . . Do you not understand me . . .?
I'm afraid I . . .
(*Breaks in, arms flying in the air*) I'M NOT AFRAID OF—— WORK I'M NOT AFRAID OF WORK AND NEVER WAS . . . but it's waiting around like this . . . and then, when you have to be as good as the next man Now do you see?
Oh yes, yes indeed.
Turf! (*Spits. Nods across shoulder.*) Turf! Yyyyatch!
Yes indeed, turf.
(*Whirls around opening mouth, eyes, ears and nose simultaneously full out.*) I've worked on the City of Dublin and the City of Glasgow . . . I've worked in Liverpool . . . I'VE WORKED ABOVE IN THE QUAYS AND ALL THE TIME YOU HAD TO BE AS GOOD AS THE NEXT MAN . . . I'VE WORKED ON THE BOATS . . . Digging COAL, COAL. But the crowd there (*nods over the shoulder*)! I've worked and I've dug coal and there that time I was over in Glasgow I worked all the time and there was no

time I wasn't working from the time I left till the time I came back . . .

It must have been pretty tough . . .

Tough? TOUGH? What are you talking about? You were working there . . . and you didn't sweat unless the next man sweat now do you see?

Yes.

You had to work all the time and you had to be as good as the next man. Sure what am I talking about, wasn't I earning nine pounds a week there . . . WASN'T I!

Yes indeed, oh yes.

(*Quiet warm ooze of memory.*) I wasn't married then, of course. But she's dead now the poor girl is dead and buried and I have one little girl and thank God she doesn't want for anything. SHE DOESN'T WANT FOR ANYTHING.

No indeed, why should she?

Hah? Hah? Oh yes . . . (*Musing.*) You shovelled coal and you worked and you were as good as the next man but that crowd over there THEY DON'T KNOW A HA'PORTH ABOUT IT. *Unloading . . . turf!* And the grumbles of them! Listen to me, me man, I'd like to see that crowd trying to dig coal! They couldn't begin to look at it THEY COULDN'T BEGIN TO LOOK AT IT THE UNIONS HAS THEM SPILED THEY'RE NOT THE MEN THEIR FATHERS WERE THEY DON'T KNOW WHAT IT IS TO WORK AND WORK AND WORK AND ALL THE TIME BE AS GOOD AS THE NEXT MAN. Now do you see what I mean?

Yes. I think I must be off now.

Hah? Hah? HAH?

Entre messire Milezio Gopallini sénateur, richement vêtu d'une robe de brocart rouge à grands ramages verts et jaunes, une chaîne d'or au cou, et tenant à la main sa barrette de velours noir entourée d'un cordon de grosses perles, beau visage, très brun, cheveux noirs coupés courts, longue barbe noire frisée, boucles d'oreilles en rubis. Il ferme la porte violemment.

FRA BARTOLOMMEO DI SAN MARCO: Toi, par ton étalage de velours et de broderies par tes plumes et ton poignard doré et tes bagues, tu insultes à la misère de tes frères!

GOPALLINI: De mes frères? *De mes frères?* (*Turns white-faced to readers.*) Est-ce vous tous, canailles, qui auriez l'impudence de vous intituler mes frères? D'ici là, il se passera de temps! Mes frères sont morts!!! C'étaient les artistes de l'ancienne Rome!!!!

Cris de terreur et grand mouvement dans la foule, qui sort. Enter a secretary bearing a copy of the Irish Times *on a velvet cushion embroidered with human ears, ceiling roses, fleur de Leix and purple wistaria.*

SECRETARY: Your paper, Excellency . . .

GOPALLINI (*screaming*): It's not my paper! It belongs to that other crowd! Did you mark these things?

SECRETARY: Of a surety, Excellency.

GOPALLINI: Well go on, what are you staring at? Read them out.

SECRETARY: Some of them are pretty tough, I am afraid, Your Majesty. You see . . . it was a Saturday issue . . .

GOPALLINI: *Tod und Teufel! Ruhleben und Drang nach Austin einen Tag um den andern!* Go on!

SECRETARY: 'Two Minutes To Season Green Timber.'

GOPALLINI: That's due to atomic lethargy—go on.

SECRETARY: Thank you, sir. 'Crying "Less politeness to monsters" she inflicted a deep but not fatal wound . . .'

GOPALLINI: Carry on, I'm listening.

SECRETARY: 'Hats have seldom been prettier than this year.'—Mr Randolph Churchill.

GOPALLINI: Whose hats? The daddy's? And what's pretty about this year that hats should be prettier than it?

SECRETARY: 'He has been absorbed into the omphalo-skeptic sense of the group . . .'

GOPALLINI: Musha, if that isn't a precise and delicate image! Here, give it to me. 'The potable alcohol in what ever quantities it is required. It will most probably be used for perfumes, cosmetics, medicinal and other purposes . . .' Too right—but there's wan place you won't see it and that's on the mahogany in front of you—gone are the days when publicans offered you potables . . . to drink. 'Varnish, diluted liquid stockings or leg paint, extract of humus and nostrums for sheep scab *are not potables* and should not be called whiskey or brandy, mark that carefully.' (Did anything come of that scheme for starting a potable typewriter factory?) 'If the United Nations are wise, they will let Spain stew in her own juice . . .' Ah yes, that's good. It's really a short way of saying that the best thing ever happened a neuthrial is for the hewin' eye-tied ignatians to fire her government and send in the travelling saints of UNNRA to take over (or just to take). It's a way of saying this most funny thing, viz. that the political programme of the United Nations and her two allies, U.S.A. and the British Empire (i.e. Communism) is what's good for people only they are too stupid to see it. Or, alternatively, it's a way of praising the scheme whereby American schoolteachers are to be sent to Europe to instruct certain nations there in civilisation, i.e. the American Way of Life. Here's a bit about William Joyce: 'That a man charged with a grave political offence should be tried publicly before an experienced judge, in an atmosphere of rigorous impartiality, and have his case twice re-investigated on appeal, are things over which we in this country might ponder . . .' Note that 'we in this country', racked by inexperienced, biased judges, steeped in an atmosphere of unrigorous (or pliant) partiality do not include in our numbers Mr William Joyce, who lost his life owing to attending a war trial.

I am far too old and wise to be aware of time in the ordinary cycle of human apprehension, so I cannot say how long ago it was since the august Nuremberg trials began. But there will be plenty to ponder over after all the defendants there arraigned have their cases twice investigated on appeal. Secretary!

SECRETARY: I am here, sir, Your Highness.

GOPALLINI: Please make a note: tell all Irish newspaper editors that the Head wishes to see them in his study at ten p.m. tomorrow morning.

The following 'conversation' took place the other evening in a well-known Dublin restaurant and was taken down by me verbatim, courtesy of Sir Isaac Pitman.

DINER: Have you a me and you?

WAITER: Pairdin?

DINER: Is there no me and you in the place?

WAITER: Oh sairtintly sir. (*Hands over card.*)

D. (*musing*): I wonder what we'll have today at all. I think we'll try the horse dovers.

W.: Sairtintly sir.

D.: Hould your horses now for a minit. What's all *this* about?

W.: That sir? That's what we call the hoofs poesh bene-dicteen, a very tasty dish sir. Eggs.

D.: EGGS? Surely to God you're not going to tell me this is Friday? (*Consults evening paper.*) Wake up man—this is Thursday.

W.: Sairtintly this is Thursday.

D.: Have you any tamata soup at all?

W.: Sairtintly we have.

D.: Hould your horses for a minit now. Wait till we see what we're going to have. (*Looks up.*) Do you know what I'm going to tell you? I'm famished with the hunger. Out all last night with a certain party if you understand me. Eggs? Oh not damn likely. What I'm going to have here and now is a right feed for myself and if wan isn't enough to fill me it'll be ditto macanaspey again. Do you get me?

W.: I understand you sir. What about a steak?

D.: Powl. Pow let rotty. What's this thing down here? Powlet.

W.: I wouldn't recommend that at all sir. It's supposed to be chicken. I seen some of it.

D.: I see. Fair enough. Hould your horses now. Horses dovers for a start. Then a drop of the tamata. Is the rolls fresh?

W.: Made this morning sir.

D.: In me eye this morning but they'll have to do. By gob do you know what it is, when you're hungry it's the divil to know what to eat. I'd eat a dead Christian Brother at the present moment. I see there's sole to be had. No good to me at all, I was never a man for fish. Wait now till we see. Hould your horses like a good man.

W.: Sairtintly. Take your time now.

D.: I'd give me eyes for bacon and cabbage.

W.: Pairdin?

D.: Be the gob I would.

W.: I see. If you look down there you will find that we have a jambone de pay ose epinard.

D.: Is that so? And who might *he* be when he's at home?

W.: Ham.

D.: *Ham.* You know what to do with *that* if you'll excuse
me saying so. What's this thing I see, here—saumon grillee?
Holy wars, a grill would be the man.

W.: That's salmon sir.

D.: Fish *again*? There's more fish on this card than in the
say if you ask me. Hould your horses for a second now.
Whisht for a second.

W.: What about a point steak borderlays?

D.: Now you're talking. I think I'll have that and a drop
of tamata.

W.: Will you have any lay gooms sir?

D.: Pairdin.

W.: Lay gooms. We have petty poys down here. Or boiled
oginons.

D.: Pairdin?

W.: Or would you prefer the steak on its own. Well done
or underdone sir?

D.: I needn't tell you I'm not supposed to eat meat at all.
The heart. You can do what you like and it's your own
business, says he, but if you go on eating red meat and drinking malt, you'll drop dead any minute. That's me last warning, says he to me, don't say I didn't tell you after you're
dead. He put the heart across me. Is that so, doctor, says I.
And would you tell me what's the good of being alive at all if
you can't drink or have a dacent meal. I thought you said,
says he, that you had a wife and fambily? Sairtintly I have,
says I. Well would you not think of others for a change for
wanst, says he. *Sairtintly* I would, says I—who said I
wouldn't? The cheek of some of them fellas is nobody's
business. Mind yourself now, don't work too hard, don't
worry and please give me four guineas. For putting a stato-
scope on my chest. Do I this and do I that? Oh yes, every
morning doctor. Sairtintly. A right crowd if you like. It
would take you a half an hour to walk past the cars some of
them have. You mustn't under any circumstances touch malt,
says he, it'll kill you in the end and the next night what do I
see but my nabs being carted out of a sairtin club in Stephen's
Green plastered to the world and lurried into a taxi. I'll go
bail he had about eighteen steaks in him as well.

W.: They do be in here an odd time.

D.: Keep far away from them now. Lave them alone. All the same, maybe I'd better forget about that steak. The meat isn't hung right in these places. The wife is a great cook. Do you know what she does with a steak first and foremost.

W.: What?

D.: Gives it an unmerciful hiding with a poker. In the name of God, says I, what are you doing that for. *That'll make the toughest steak tender*, says she. Give that tip to the crowd in the kitchen here. Do you know what I think I'll have? A damn good feed of bacon and eggs.

W.: *Pairdin?*

D.: With tea. Real tea, scalding hot.

W.: I see.

D.: And some nice white rolls, and bags of butter. And I needn't tell you what we'll have while we're waiting.

W.: What would that be sir?

D.: A drop of the tamata, of course.

W.: Sairtintly sir.

D.: What'll all that run me?

W.: Fifteen and eightpence sir.

D.: Fifteen and *whatpence?* Fifteen and EIGHTPENCE? Ah well (*very low sad voice*) if I look like one it can't be helped, God's will be done, but let me out of here before I get excited, and it cost me four guineas to be told never to do that.

W.: Very good sir.

D.: Very good me fut.

(*Departs, struggling into overcoat en route.*)

The District and Other Courts

Mr Myles na gCopaleen, who gave his address as Westmoreland Street, Dublin, and described himself as 'the grand old Irish man', appeared on 492 currency charges at Bow Street, London, yesterday. He was fined a total of £2,350,000 and ordered to pay £6 5s 6d expenses. A beautiful creature attired in furs, who gave her name as Yvonne Desirée Lebaisir, was bound to the peace for aiding and abetting. She described herself as 'a former member of the Résistance'.

Mr Gerald Cockshott, prosecuting, said that a Treasury agent who was investigating currency transactions on the Continent was accosted by the male accused in the bar of the Hotel Carlton at Cannes and asked whether he would mind cashing in francs a cheque for £500,000. Accused added that he would give the Treasury agent 'a monkey for himself'. When the latter revealed his identity, the accused apologised and gave particulars of over four hundred other cheques he had already cashed. Accused also showed the stub of his cheque book, which indicated that cheques totalling some two million pounds had been drawn in favour of Max Intrator. Accused characterised his own behaviour as 'incredibly naïve and stupid and out of all harmony with the fundamental considerations' and expressed his readiness to return to Britain, by air if necessary, 'to face the music'. He permitted himself to say that possibly Miss Lebaisir was 'not incapable of extravagant attitudes'. Counsel understood that defendant had some standing as a statesman in Ireland but otherwise was not known to have criminal associations. The Treasury was pressing for the most exemplary penalties.

Mr Maurice Maul, for the defendant, said that his client, who was the famous author, could have pleaded diplomatic immunity, but, scorning such a course, actually insisted on the strictest examination of his affairs by the court. The law was the law but each one in court, in whatever interest bound, would have his own opinions as to the merits of a process whereby a gallant fighter pilot of the R.A.F. found himself in the dock for innocently indulging the same selfless impulses which made him answer the call when Britain was in distress. He did not think it would be disputed that defendant had brought down 312 machines during the war.

MAGISTRATE: What sort of machines?

COUNSEL: On that point my brief is silent.

MAGISTRATE: If you wish to present an attested military record by way of character, do so.

COUNSEL: My instructions are to attempt nothing of the kind.

Proceeding, he said defendant had travelled to the Continent on urgent national business, and it became necessary to have Miss Lebaisir in his suite. Miss Lebaisir was by profession a nurse.

MAGISTRATE: Whom does this lady nurse?

COUNSEL: The defendant, I understand.

Defendant, in evidence, said he went to France on a secret political mission which would not be 'in anybody's interest to discuss'. It was true that Miss Lebaisir was a nurse and had on occasions satisfactorily nursed himself, but her main business was to be seen with him in public, owing to her costly appearance. It was his experience that it was impossible for a man to look costly in public by himself. It was necessary to be accompanied by a costly-looking lady. Then it was easy.

MAGISTRATE: What was easy?

DEFENDANT: The game I was at.

Continuing, defendant said that the cheques which the Treasury complained of arose through thoughtlessness on his part. Some strangers whom he met in the hotel bar told him they had been unlucky at the tables, and asked for the loan of a million pounds. He had, foolishly perhaps, given them three-quarters of a million. It appeared that unfortunately their luck did not turn and he felt that he had no option but to advance them further monies, possibly another million. On the instructions of the men he made the cheques out to Mr Max Intrator, for whose co-operation he was obliged. The half a million he asked the Treasury officer to get him was to cover his travelling expenses home. He now realised that he had acted foolishly and impulsively and was prepared to pay such monetary penalties as the Treasury might demand. He asked that there should be no question of jail, as he was not the jail-going type.

The Magistrate imposed the fines stated, without comment. Defendant immediately paid by cheque and left the court.

(NOTE: Defendant was subsequently re-arrested on the instructions of the Treasury, who found his cheque was worthless, but was later quietly released when it was found that all cheques issued in the case were also worthless and that Mr Max Intrator had probably been badly stung. Defendant, on reaching Collinstown, was entertained to a banquet by Aer Lingus.)

When the further hearing of the charges against M. Copaleen was resumed in the District Court yesterday, a high official of Radio Eireann was called. He stated he was blocking a post, was on his max, and denied that he had any grievances when questioned on the subject by the accused.

DEFENDANT: Do you ever get e'er an invitation to go on any of air jaunts, with free feeds below in Rineanna and all the rest of it?

WITNESS: No, sir.

DEFENDANT: I put it to you that that's a grievance and that you're victimised because you haven't got a black homburg and a brief case. And a silk scarf with spots in it.

WITNESS: No sir. It is not my business to deal with air matters.

DEFENDANT: I thought your Radio Eireann was on the air every night? (*Laughter.*)

JUSTICE: You'd better make your questions relevant.

DEFENDANT (*to witness*): Your business then is the highly technical one of radio broadcasting. Kindly afford the court a succinct account of the training you received in radio techniques at British, American or Continental broadcastings before entering on your present employment.

WITNESS: None, sir.

DEFENDANT: You realise that that answer vitiates your testimony as a purported expert in these matters. Can you converse in the Irish tongue?

WITNESS: *Tá.* (*Laughter.*)

SUPERINTENDENT: Your Worship, I protest against this! He is trying to humiliate and brow-beat this gentleman.

JUSTICE: I have already issued one warning.

DEFENDANT (*after studying his papers, said*): This mysterious business of the broken gramophone records. You visited the scene of the crime with high-ranking policemen?

WITNESS: I did. I was one of the first on the scene.

DEFENDANT: And there you perceived a record, badly smashed. Kindly tell the court in your own words what was the name of the record.

WITNESS: The record was 'The Blue Danube'.

DEFENDANT: I see. (*Here defendant looked very meaningfully around the court and paused for a long time, studying papers. At last he again addressed the witness.*) I see. Tell me ... have you travelled much throughout the world?

WITNESS: I was in London and Dundee.

DEFENDANT (*after pause*): London and Dundee? Then it is true to say that the spacious continent of Europe was, in its heyday, unknown to you?

WITNESS: Only from story books, sir.

DEFENDANT: To come back to this record of 'The Blue Danube'. Would you please tell the court HOW MANY TIMES IT WAS PLAYED OVER YOUR RADIO DURING THE LAST YEAR!!

WITNESS: I have the figure here. It was played 4,312 times in all. About twelve times every day of the year.

DEFENDANT: I see. I trust the court has noted that reply. I trust the reply is carefully noted.

JUSTICE: I ... I thought it was oftener ...

DEFENDANT (*to witness*): Have you ever heard of Vienna?

WITNESS: I have.

DEFENDANT: No doubt the term 'Wienerwald' is familiar to you?

WITNESS: I never heard tell of that, sir.

DEFENDANT: Very well. Let me put it to you this way: Vienna is a large city, now architecturally somewhat passé but of natural surroundings and siting still among the first on earth. It touches upon the Danube, in German known as the Donau, already mentioned in these proceedings. It boasts, however, of another impressive natural feature. HAVE YOU EVER HEARD OF THE VIENNA WOODS?

WITNESS: Yes, sir. (*Here witness asked for a glass of water.*)

JUSTICE (*warmly*): Now I think we are getting somewhere!

DEFENDANT (*to witness*): Certain legends are associated with these woods. A foreign gentleman named Strauss has purported to make these legends the subject of a banal and infuriating musical composition. It is called 'Tales from the Vienna Woods'. HAVE YOU EVER HEARD OF IT?

WITNESS: I have. That was the name of the other record smashed in the studio.

DEFENDANT: How many times was that one broadcast last year?

WITNESS: 6,835 times, sir.

Defendant, addressing the court, said that while the guilt of any individual for breaking the law had not been established, it was plain that the situation reeked of superhuman provocation. The most law-abiding man must not be tried too hard. He asked for a direction.

The Justice, speaking with emotion, said that he would refuse informations. His own home had been broken up and his family scattered owing to certain matters mentioned in court. He would not, however, obtrude personal issues on what was a judicial finding. He allowed defendant his costs. Subsequently the Justice had a seizure in his room.

The Editor has learned with regret that Mr Myles na gCopaleen has been again before the District Court, having been arrested near Leixlip in company with a woman of the Gipsy class. The hearing was in camera but it is understood that he was charged with the larceny of four bicycle tyres and a tram. (We suspect this last is a telegraphic error for 'pram'.) Both accused were sentenced to fourteen days with hard labour and it is unlikely that Mr na gCopaleen's notes will appear in these columns for a fortnight. We regret very much the inconvenience to our readers.

An unusual application came before the High Court yesterday when a minor who gave his name as Myles na gCopaleen applied for permission to marry without the consent of his parents or guardians. Appellant was a person of low size, attired in a suit of black velvet but was bandaged about the face, making his age and expression somewhat indefinite. For some reason there was a large force of Guards present. A member of the court invited him to come down from the witness box, not to be shy or afraid, and to sit at the solicitors' table.

APPELLANT: You are indeed kind to me, sir.

JUDGE: Now my little man, tell us all about it. We are all here to help you. Our only aim is to make you happy.

APPELLANT: Sir, you are indeed kind.

JUDGE: Tell us, now—what age are you?

APPELLANT: I am but ten, sir.

JUDGE: *Ten?* Goodness gracious, surely it is very early for you to be thinking of marriage? Ten?

APPELLANT: Sir, if youth be a sin, then I confess it is a sin to which I am committed. But, good sir, bear with me please, for one brief hour. I aspire to the sacred office of husband and father.

JUDGE: But you are only a child! Whom do you wish to marry?

APPELLANT: Ah, kind sir, I have not yet spoken, not yet dared utter, the dear wishes of my heart in the ear of the lady who has wrung the sweet tribute of passionate love from me. To speak her name in this place, sir—'twere to take a liberty alien to the usages of gentlemen, however young. Pray forgive me, sir, but her name—that I cannot tell.

JUDGE: Can you write?

APPELLANT: But poorly, sir.

JUDGE: Then write her name down on a piece of paper. Nobody but myself and the other judges will know.

Appellant laboriously wrote down a name and the paper was handed up to the bench.

APPELLANT: I love her dearly, sir.

JUDGE: How long have you known this lady?

APPELLANT: Sir, we were childhood sweethearts.

JUDGE: How long have you known her?

APPELLANT: Sir, I dare not to living mortal divulge the exact date or time, for e'en yet I have not taken action about the matter of my troth.

JUDGE: Your troth?

APPELLANT: Kind sir, I have not yet plighted it.

(A Guard was heard to observe: Begob it's the hairy ten years of age. I never seen more cheek and cod in me life, a person that was doin' the three cards in Naas when I was stationed below there as a Free State Army private in nineteen and twenty-six and that's not today nor yesterday.)

JUDGE: I must say this is an extraordinary application.

APPELLANT: I am a lifelong abstainer.

JUDGE: Have we any evidence of character?

Sir Myles na gCopaleen (the da), giving evidence, said that in his experience appellant was a very respectable man.

JUDGE: A respectable *man?*

WITNESS: Bedad I suppose you would call him that.

JUDGE: Is he at school or does he work?

WITNESS: I never seen him doing a hand's turn. All the same, he talks a lot about work. One time he was all for starting a thing that he says is badly wanted in this country, a laundry for soiled bibs.

JUDGE: I see?

WITNESS: Another time he was all for doing something about the copybooks.

JUDGE: What copybooks?

WITNESS: The blots, you know. He was for getting out some patent, some de-inking business for persons in this country that has blotted the copybooks. There's a great number of copybooks in need of attention. Between some of the justices flying to the bottle too often and——

JUDGE: That's quite enough! Have you anything further to say on the question of character?

WITNESS: Nothing, except that the applicant is a thoroughly honest, trustworthy married man, a man of sterling character, honest as the day is long and as straight as a die.

JUDGE: If the man is married, the application fails.

APPELLANT: It's illegal for a person of my age to be married, kind sir.

JUDGE (*to older man*): You'd better bring this child of yours away as quickly as possible. The whole thing savours of contempt.

SIR MYLES (the da): A nod is as good as a wink. Thank you sir.

(Father and son then left the court, the latter crying loudly.)

On the resumption of the proceedings in the District Court against M. Copaleen, alias 'Tarzan' of the Animal Gang (reported in yesterday's *Irish Times*), many hundreds of people in the court were wearing headphones, and brilliant arc-lights flooded the shabby court-room. Defendant lounged in the dock, saluting various friends in the gallery. The Justice, taking his seat, said he would tolerate no disorder.

DEFENDANT: I got a hiding off the Guards last night. I was beaten up and made kiss the toes of a blackguard from Skibbereen that was a sergeant in nineteen and twenty-four but reduced to the ranks for drink, a *grauchalogue* of a Kerry bosthoon! Is that justice?

SUPERINTENDENT: I will deal with these allegations in their place. It will be shown that since the last meeting of the court, one of our men is disabled for life.

JUSTICE: Very well. I will now hear evidence. This is a very serious charge—breaking into the Post Office. We want no irrelevancies or red herrings . . .

DEFENDANT: Such an idea of exclusivism is incompatible with justice, being alien to reason. Even minute details contribute to the content of judicial fact. A judge should be an exceptional person, not the tool of ephemeral political creeds: *not*, certainly, a member of the mentally confined herds mentioned by Tullius Cicero (in his *Academicorum Priorum Liber II*, of course) when he referred to *multi qui omnino Graecas non ament litteras, plures qui philosophiam, reliqui, etiam si haec non improbent, tamen earum rerum disputationem principibus civitatis non ita decoram putant*. Upon my word I'll——

SUPERINTENDENT: Your Worship——

JUSTICE: Go ahead, Superintendent. I'll keep my temper!

The Superintendent said that the charges referred to an attack made by the defendant on the Radio Eireann broadcasting station. Doors and locks were prised open with chisels or blunt instruments, valuable gramophone records were wantonly smashed and a lady's handbag, the property of a member of the orchestra, was slashed. Defendant was arrested on the roof of the G.P.O. where he was found in possession of a parcel.

DEFENDANT: Tell the whole truth. What was in the parcel?

SUPERINTENDENT: Six stouts.

DEFENDANT: Did I tell you that I had an appointment earlier in the evening at the corner of Hawkins Street with a man from Edenderry and that he gave me the parcel to mind for him?

SUPERINTENDENT: You did. You also said you had not been in Parnell Street for six years. You were observed in a licensed premises in Parnell Street from four till eight-thirty on the day in question.

DEFENDANT: Was I alone there if I was there at all?

SUPERINTENDENT: That question is irrelevant.

JUSTICE: You might as well answer. This'll be all splashed in the papers.

SUPERINTENDENT: There was a senator with you. And two ladies.

DEFENDANT: Now it is coming out! Did we then proceed to a licensed premises in Capel Street?

SUPERINTENDENT: You did.

DEFENDANT: Since you know so much, kindly tell the court what we had there.

SUPERINTENDENT: The testimony of the foreman is that the ladies had sherry-wines and that the gentlemen had 'scoops'.

DEFENDANT: Did the foreman refuse to serve me later, after I had smashed a glass?

JUSTICE (*to defendant*): If this is a drink alibi, you will not get away with it, I'll warrant you that!

DEFENDANT (*to Superintendent*): Was I later observed seated in an armchair in a secondhand clothes shop in Camden Street?

SUPERINTENDENT: You dodged in there all right!

Defendant, addressing the court, asked for a direction. There was absolutely no case to answer. He would not go so far as to say that he was never in the G.P.O. in his life—that were to invite the perversion of history—but inasmuch as he had pleaded not guilty to the fantastic charges before the court, it would be a prostitution of the organs of justice towards base ends if the case was proceeded with.

JUSTICE: We'll risk that.

Defendant pointed out that he had a British Army pension which would be forfeited in the event of a conviction.

JUSTICE: You should have thought of that before you tried to disable the radio station.

Proceeding.

Yesterday in the District Court, an elderly shabbily clad man, whose name was given as M. Copaleen, was put forward on the charge that he did, in company with a person or persons unknown, damage several locks, doors and glass panels in the G.P.O. premises, that he broke into the premises and wilfully destroyed certain phonographic material valued at 23/6d. Defendant refused to remove his cap on entering the dock.

JUSTICE: Take that man's hat off!

The cap was forcibly removed by a Gárda.

DEFENDANT: *O vale, pileole vetuste!*

A Garda superintendent said that this was the defendant's fifth appearance before the court; he was an habitual criminal with a long list of convictions in Sheffield and Swansea and gave the police a lot of trouble——

DEFENDANT (*interrupting*): *Moi d'abord!*

JUSTICE: What do you mean?

DEFENDANT: The so-called court has not thought fit to inquire whether or not I plead guilty. Does your Holy Worship's political pedigree make it unnecessary for you to observe the British legal rituals?

JUSTICE (*glowering*): Do you plead guilty or not guilty?

DEFENDANT (*in a loud voice*): *Ich bekenne mich nicht schuldig. Vor Gott und vor——*

JUSTICE: You will make no speeches here or give me any of your impudence! And we want none of your languages out of you either——

DEFENDANT: *O tá go maith. Maith go leor má's seadh. Laidean agus teangthacha nea-Shacsanacha nach í annso feasta. Seasaim ar an Bhunreacht!*

JUSTICE: What'd he say?

SUPERINTENDENT: He said it'd be all Latin now. He says he has his rights.

At this stage an impressive-looking stranger rose and conversed with the Superintendent. He then asked the Justice whether, in the interest of justice, he might be heard?

JUSTICE: Who are *you*?

DEFENDANT (*to stranger*): Gob I seen *you* before.

The Stranger said that he was Mr Justice Jackson. He had passed through Rineanna while on brief furlough from his exertions at Nuremberg. He had visited the court that morning merely to study Irish legal forms; he had no connection with the case.

The Justice said it was a great honour to welcome so distinguished an American jurist to the court; he was sure his legal colleagues in court joined with him in that welcome. He felt that he was also on safe ground when he said that they in Ireland were proud, and justifiably proud of the airport at which their distinguished guest had first put his foot on Irish soil——

DEFENDANT (*to Justice Jackson*): Have you been above in the Park yet?

JUSTICE: Our airport at Rineanna is something of which we are definitely proud.

Mr Justice Jackson said that Shannon Airport was a tribute to Irish brains and foresight. What he had seen there impressed him very much. He was received there with great courtesy. He also wished to pay tribute to the Ennis Chamber of Commerce, which placed a car at his disposal and entertained him to a banquet. He had also had the good fortune to meet Mr de Valera, for whom he had always entertained a warm admiration. He was much impressed with Mr de Valera's sincerity——

DEFENDANT: *Conspice, O Constellatio alata, me—— perduellionis scelere constrictum, muryaa! Inter verba silent leges!*

Mr Justice Jackson said that his sole reason for intervening in the proceedings was the similarity he discerned as between the conduct of the accused and the war criminals at Nuremberg. The latter, particularly Streicher, Goering and Ribbentrop, had given a lot of trouble. They insisted on speaking German instead of English. It was tempting to take a sum-mary course in such circumstances but that would be alien to American justice. Instead, they had installed a multi-lingual headphone system which had removed the discord of language difficulties. He strongly recommended the present court to adopt a similar course.

The Justice warmly thanked Mr Jackson and adjourned the court to enable this to be done.

DEFENDANT (*leaving dock*): I'm going to get rough below in the cells!

Proceeding.

I was up before Judge Shannon the other morning. However, we won't go into that now, as Evans of the Broke wittily remarked to his fellow passengers as they stood regarding the sea from the deck of the *Bolivar*. We have other matters to att-10-d 2, all manner of important matters. (What—you're curious about my being up before George Shannon? Well, I will tell you about it some time, but not now, *nunc non occasio est nec tempus*, other matters, of import most exigent, make urgent call upon our proper consideration.) (But this one question I will put you—is it *illegal* for me to get up at 5 a.m. for some skipping and roadwork if, simultaneously, George Shannon remains abed?)

Some time ago the Irish Times, Limited, was proceeded against in the District Court. I managed to get a copy of the reporter's transcript of the proceedings before the original was mysteriously 'lost'. The company was charged with cruelty to Myles na gCopaleen, overworking him, working while in an unfit condition, failing to have him properly shod, and neglecting to feed him. The case, enough to make one's blood bile, was kept out of the papers at the time, witnesses were hushed up, bribes changed hands and, for myself, I was as good as offered my passage to South America. (But Perón had a word to say there!) Let me quote from the suppressed newspaper report:

A Guard deposed that on receiving a report from an inspector of N.S.P.C.A., he examined Myles na gCopaleen, who was in a distressed condition. He had two sores the size of half-crowns under his collar, one of his shoes was falling off. He was in a spavined condition and was limping badly. A veterinary surgeon

who subsequently examined him ordered him to be destroyed.
Irish Times representatives undertook to do this themselves however. He last saw Myles na gCopaleen being conveyed up the
quays in a float . . .

(Mark well that this happened on a Thursday, *in the same
week* in which I had given Austin and Seumas my word of
honour as a gentleman that I would attend the PEN above in
Jury's on Saturday where they were throwing a dinner for
me!)

(*Memo: Literary Conundrum:* What is it which, when a
gentleman gives he always keeps? Answer, his word!)

On the point of overworking, harrowing evidence was
given by a lady inspector of Myles na gCopaleen being
worked by a member of the *Irish Times* editorial staff. Myles
was at that time in an unfit condition. The bully had him
wedged into the wall near Webb's bookshop and was working
him very hard, compelling him to write stuff on the backs of
envelopes. The report continues:

JUSTICE: Was he being beaten?

WITNESS: He was getting an odd quiet kick for himself. But
there was mental cruelty also. He was being made to write Latin
in the street when it was freezing to see whether he could do it
without his dictionaries.

JUSTICE: *O scelestum ac nefarium facinus!*
(*Laughter.*)

WITNESS: His little face was all blue.

Further evidence showed that Myles na gCopaleen was
regularly worked with undue severity 'in a certain establishment' with nothing 'before him bar a small port and peppermint'. Four of his chilblains were open at the material times.
The Company denied starving Myles na gCopaleen and a
stable employee swore that on a day when it was alleged no
food had been provided for Myles na gCopaleen, 'a feed of
boxty' had been 'fired into him' at four o'clock.

There is any amount more of horrifying detail, but I think
I have given enough to show how Ireland treats her literary
men. And do not for a moment imagine I am the only one.
Wheeled hearses would not induce me to mention names but
readers may well ask themselves why it is that P. S. O'Heg-

arty, our inimitable Cass&rus, grows daily more gloomy, more displeased with the future. (Rather unIrish attitude, that—being displeased with the past was good enough for our forefathers.) Next thing you know, the few of us who are Left—philosophers, poets, artists, call us what you will—will be beyond on the Third Programme as God apparently intended. Poets have been called the Anthony of a nation. Sorry, antennae. They look like becoming postnnae in this poor land. Contrast the treatment (the next two words follow quite naturally) *meted out* to us with the sumptuous rewards which in bounteous deluge fall upon the writers of cheap fiction such as adventure stories, detective stories, Government 'white papers' and the like, with slim English actors coming across to take part in the films of them! Crime does not pay, they say. Pay whom? Did it pay Edgar Wallace? They say that racing is a mug's game. Did Nat Gould find it so?

There is only one solution for this situation: our excellent Government will have to introduce a Civil List to sustain such of our poets, dramatists and artists who, through motives of artistic integrity and pride, persist in being high-class Irish literary men. A token vote of £1,000,000 would do the trick for what remains of the present financial year.

Otherwise ... well, I have pointed to the danger. Our artists will compromise with Mammon and pollute themselves with the lucre attaching to murder and race-course 'thrillers'. They will go where the money is. *All that glisters is Nat Gould!*

(NOTE: The author stoutly denies that the entirety of the foregoing article, which has been suppressed by the *Irish Times*, was written for the purposes of the last sentence.)

A scene which took place on the Dublin Quays on Monday last had a sequel in the District Court when a poorly clad elderly man who gave his name as Myles Choplin, alias Keoghesy, alias Coplin, was charged with conduct likely to lead to a breach of the peace; he was also charged with resisting arrest and using bad language.

A Detective Sergeant said that a number of persons saw a boy climb on the river wall and fall into the water. A small crowd collected and an unknown young man dived fully clothed to the rescue. He succeeded in bringing the boy to a ladder and willing helpers assisted rescuer and rescued to the street. The latter was semi-conscious and artificial respiration was applied. In the prevailing excitement the heroic young man disappeared. While the boy was being revived a scene was caused by the defendant.

JUSTICE: How?

SERGEANT: He accosted a number of spectators and asked for glasses of malt.

JUSTICE: No doubt the poor man was unnerved by the occurrence. (*Laughter.*)

Continuing, the Sergeant said that defendant was a notorious waster. Two witnesses would be produced to prove that after the boy had been recovered from the water, defendant entered an adjacent knacker's yard and poured a bucket of water over his head. Shortly later he was observed sitting in a horse-trough. The purpose of these antics would not be lost on the court. He (the defendant) did not hesitate to sully the scene of a gallant deed by a despicable display of obstruction and begging coupled with the suggestion that the defendant had a claim on the crowd's sympathy by reason of being implicated in the rescue, if not being solely responsible for it. He also damaged the clothing of members of the crowd by moving among them with his wet clothes.

JUSTICE: You mean he wet the people with his wet clothes?

SERGEANT: It was worse than that. The man was festooned be knackers' offals.

At this point defendant replaced his cap on his head. It was immediately removed by a Guard.

SERGEANT: He plastered four people's clothes with blood with ferocious thing that was hanging out of him from the knacker's yard. He had them button-holed and him asking for the whiskey.

JUSTICE: Did he get whiskey?

SERGEANT: He did not.

JUSTICE: And what did he do then?

SERGEANT: He threw a fit for himself.

Continuing, the Sergeant said that when defendant 'collapsed' in the middle of the crowd a number of well-meaning people, unaware of his character, rushed to his assistance and applied artificial respiration. At least one man left the half-drowned boy to do this. When defendant was 'revived' he shouted to the crowd to look after the boy first. Subsequently he asked for a glass of brandy, inviting a bystander to 'send up to Keogh's for it'.

DEFENDANT: *O miseri! O miserrimi!*

The Sergeant said that when an ambulance arrived for the boy, defendant endeavoured to cause himself to be carried into it. He was ejected by the attendants and then lay down in the gutter. He began shouting to the crowd.

JUSTICE: Shouting about what?

SERGEANT: Drink. The ante was down be that time. He was ready to settle for a pint at the heel of the hunt. When I cautioned him he asked me 'was this treatment for heroes?' When I went to arrest him, he shouted to the crowd to rescue him. I gave a half an hour trying to get him up offa the ground.

DEFENDANT: I was too weak to stand but I got a hidin' off you.

JUSTICE: What do you mean?

DEFENDANT: Your man gave me a right box and me below on the ground. I have a complete answer to these charges. Remand me on bail to the Supreme Court. I know Tim.

JUSTICE: I will adjourn this case till tomorrow. If you have any answers to these charges you had better have them ready.

DEFENDANT: As a monarchist I recognise this court.

Defendant was carried below by Guards and the day's proceedings terminated.

Bores

Early morning workers passing by my lodgings on Monday probably heard two volleys. Actually I had my firing squad at work in my yard. Two base types who had indogged—I beg pardon—incurred my displeasure, were, at my orders, put to death.

(But first an anecdote: many years ago a friend called to see me and was good enough to inquire about my nephew, who had joined the London police as a cadet. 'And where is he now?' inquired the visitor. 'He's in the Yard,' I answered. 'Oh?' Up with your man and out, absent for fifteen minutes. Then back: 'I don't see any sign of him there.')

The two vile creatures I caused to be shot are now in their graves (*their* graves, mark you) as a warning to others. The first was *It's a Disease, You Know*.

'That man thinks, dreams, works, sleeps chess. He has a pocket set and works away at it in trains and buses. He has about thirty correspondence games going on simultaneously and is a member of four clubs.'

'It's a disease, you know.'

'So-and-so's drinking far too much. Never anything less than a large brandy and soda, popping in and out of pubs all day long, drunk night and morning, not a stitch on his back and the wife gone back to the mother.'

'It's a disease you know.'

'So-and-so's a demon for work. He works about sixteen hours a day, Sunday included, and hasn't had a holiday for eighteen years.'

'It's a disease, you know.'

'Our friend was giving out again last night about compulsory Irish. He worked himself into a fearful state—schoolchildren were being turned into illiterate clods, people were being driven from the country in tens of thousands, the latest outrage was that solicitors had to know Gaelic, to speak English would soon be a crime to be tried by the Special Court, and so on.'

'It's a disease, you know.'

It's a disease, eh? You know *him*, I'm sure. I wonder is he worse or better than the other ruffian I executed. I mean *Ah But If We All Did That*.

'Tell you an idea. Now that there's a 'flu epidemic and everybody's expected to get it, what's wrong with—well, getting it, have a good rest in bed. I know two lads that are at that game.'

'Ah, but if we all did that . . .'

'This election—I've no interest in either party, one's as bad as the other if not worse and I'm not going to bother my head voting.'

'Ah, but if we all did that . . .'

'There's a very simple way of living practically for nothing in Dublin. Get night work in a bakery or newspaper office. Work all night, have breakfast, take a walk and then when the picture houses open at two, buy a cheap seat and sleep till eleven. No rent, no rates, no overheads.'

'Ah, but if we all did that . . .'

'I don't believe in this idea of active patriotism. Personally I would refuse to fight for my country if called upon.'

'Ah, but if we all did that . . .'

Yes, there are innumerable morons moaning out that excruciating parrot-cry, polluting millions of conversations with it throughout the globe, agonisingly inserting it into all manner of decent and reasonable talk, coming out with it *even when I am* present!

It's a disease, you know.

You recall The Man with the Watch, The Man with the Razor Blade? Would you like me to record some more pests? How about, for example, The Man Who Knows That Hitler/ Hirohito/Roosevelt/Churchill/de Valera Is *Really* Dead and What You And I See Is Only A Double? Did you ever meet that dreadful spook? (Or have I said the wrong thing—how could you meet yourself?)

Anyway, here is one you *have* met. There are at least one million of them in Ireland. I refer to The Man Who Does Not Believe That Jobs Are Obtained On Merit Or That Open Competitions For Jobs Are Genuine.

You happen to run into this person. He is unemployed and you unfortunately yield to a sentiment of pity. You say:

'I see where they're looking for a County Manager for Hy Brasil. You ought to have a shot at that, Mac—it would be just up your alley . . .'

The mouth twists into a quick smile, the hand tightens the muffler round the throat, moves up to caress the hollow stubbly cheek; the mercury eyes swerve from right to left, the tall glass of dirty fluid is bitten into and this astonishing proposition begins to be enunciated:

'I couldn't afford it . . .'

'Ah, nonsense,' you say. 'Look, if it's only a matter of two guineas, I could——'

A laugh, chilling, hollow, stops you. This is gradually stepped down to a mortuary chuckle, dissolves finally into a prim, patient smile. You are flabbergasted to perceive that you are yourself the object of pity—you, the sympathiser. Then the creature speaks:

'Two guineas? *Two guineas* . . .?'

Here there is another pause while the foul glass is emptied down the windpipe, apparently into the lungs. Terrible noises start. An embryo sneering laugh has been overtaken by a cataclysm of coughing and choking. Finally the creature again becomes articulate:

'Two guineas is good. Pay your entrance fee and take your chance, eh? Gob I'm surprised at you—a city man too!'

(That is one thing all these boys have in common—they are surprised at you—they thought you were a victim of paranoia.)

'Do you seriously mean to tell me,' the voice continues, 'that you'd have the ghost of the smell of a chance of that job barring you planked down your two fifty in Bank of England fivers? Hah? You know so-and-so? How do you suppose he got there? Hah? Oh, I could tell you stuff, I could tell you things. I could give you the surprise of your life right here where we're standing . . .'

And he does—purest of imaginative folklore.

And how about The Man Who Is Not Such A Fool As To Consult Doctors About His Ailments? 'Is it put meself into the hands of your men when I have the bread knife below on the dhresser if I want to do meself in. Does anybody know how many people is murdered in hospitals every day of the week? Stop in bed for a week now, me good man, and that'll be two guineas. *Docthors*, is it?'

Or for doctors substitute dentists:

'Oh hullo! Come in and have a tayscawn. I'm just after pulling three big molars out of the back here. Hurt? *Hurt?* Are you serious? The only way you can get teeth to hurt you is to go to the dentist . . .'

And there are plenty more of them, reader, as we shall see in a day or so.

I have been reading New York's paper *PM* (no relation to the *Saturday Evening Post Meridiem*) and therein a reverie by columnist Billy Rose. He says:

What ever happened the guy who used to read the titles out loud in the days of silent movies? To prove he could read he would repeat the titles in a voice that would shatter an eardrum at 20 paces. It seems like only last week that I sat in short pants in a neighbourhood nickelodeon and heard him nasalise: 'Came the dawn! Reginald, distraught, awoke to find Ophelia had fled.' How often I wished I were big enough to hit him on top of his pointy head!

Mr Rose does not believe that this breed has died out and after some research he has identified its present manifestations. Namely:

When it's raining cats and nanny goats, and every taxi you dash up to has a man sitting in it—that's him. When you're reading a magazine story in the dentist's office and the page with the payoff is missing—he tore it out. When you're enjoying a ringside seat in a nightclub, who bribes a waiter to put a table on the dance floor in front of you—Pointyhead. When the officious telephone operator tells you she can't return your nickel but will mail it to you in stamps—that's his sister . . .

Mr Rose identifies him with other aspects of odiousness. He gets sixty-four dollars on the radio quiz show for guessing what state New York is in. He kneels on golf courses to study a three-foot putt. And so on.

Now this wretch, described by Mr Rose, also *in Hibernia vixit*. Nowadays, what's he up to *here*?

Well, for one thing, he doesn't hire taxis—he drives them. He says that will be about eight bob. You ask to see the clock. He says the light on the clock is broken. He will see has he a match on him. He fumbles for five minutes, making sure that you will be drenched to the skin standing on the sidewalk. His match then splutters and shows that the clock says ten and sixpence. He takes your wet money and drives away without a word.

Sometimes you find him in bus queues. It is still raining. The bus is packed but there's room for one. He is the one. He is always first man on the queue. But if you manage to get on the next bus, behold—he is also there! Doing what? Whistling Toselli's serenade with vast *rubato*. You fling your newspaper, which you have read from end to end, on the floor. When you get off the bus, there is a shout behind you. You have forgotten your paper!

You have a book of sweep tickets, you have paid for it but you agree to sell one ticket. If it wins, to whom else could you have sold it? To no one but Pointyhead and you have neglected to enter your name as seller on the counterfoil.

He will gladly lend you his box of matches at a cinema show. But he is a neat and careful creature and always replaces used matches in the box. Eventually you are asked to leave the cinema for scratching dead matches to the annoyance of other patrons. When you get out, you find your hands are black.

He rings you up fourteen times on the public telephone without pressing button A and induces yourself, an adult, to shout at him to press the button, though you are thoroughly well aware he cannot hear you.

The new film you are enthusiastic about, he saw it in London two years ago. The new book, he read it in manuscript and as a matter of fact suggested a few changes.

His crowning infuriating attribute? He's successful.

There is still another monster I would like to warn you about. (To be warned is to be four-armed.) You have, very indiscreetly, complained about the price of clothes; worse, you have commented adversely on the quality of much of what is available. You see a light dawning in the monster's eye and to your alarm you realise that you are for it. Fascinated, you observe him primly take a garment he is wearing between finger and thumb. (Too late to correct the absurd ambiguity of that last sentence.) He savours the fabric appreciatively, then courteously invites you to do the same. Your fingers, hypnotised by him, obey against your own strict orders. He appears to be wearing sandpaper but your cowardice does not permit you to say this. You withdraw your hand, covertly explore your fingers for splinters, and cravenly murmur some noises of approval.

How old would you say this suit is?

You are blushing furiously now—it may be shame or anger or both—but you still dare not protest.

Would you believe me if I told you that I've that coat on me back for ten years. Know what I paid for it?

You keep on making polite noises, sorrier than ever that you were born at all.

Fifty bob!

More muttering, swallowed curses, tears.

And I'll get another ten years out of it too, you can't, do you know what it is you can't wear stuff like that out.

Let me add that this gent has a brother wants to know How Much He's Making In The Year. Go On, Tell Him, How Much Would You Say He's Making Now.

Talking again of bores, here is another Man you would want to watch:

Let us say you are poor, one meal 'does' you in the day, for smokes you rely on the cheapest cigarettes obtainable—the small hard ones sold at sixpence for ten. You chance to be in the company of this Man. You need a smoke yourself and although you cannot afford to give a single cigarette away, you have your pride and, with a shabby-genteel gesture, you offer the ruffian one. He accepts, lights up without a word, lies back in the chair and smokes in silence. You become uneasily aware that the silence is phoney—that there is something coming. Eventually, it *does*. You are flabbergasted to hear this proposition being enunciated:

'Do you know, I'm glad things is lookin' up for you again. You got it hard there for a time. I like to see a man comin' into his own. It's oney your due . . .'

'What do you mean?' you ask angrily.

'I suppose you have cleared off the debt on the house and settled a few quid on the mother. Gob it's a true thing—you can't keep a good man down.'

'I would have you know,' you shout furiously, 'that I don't know what you're talking about! It happens that I've been out of work for four years and I am kept by my uncle——'

'What!'

The loathsome oaf has sprung up in a fit of fake amazement. He stares.

'But,' he splutters, 'I don't understand. These . . . these cigarettes! How . . . how can you afford to smoke these cigarettes if you're not well-off?'

'These are the cheapest cigarettes that can be got,' you roar, walking feet first into the bear-trap. Then comes the hideous dénouement:

'Cheap? Cheap! *These?* Ho-ho, that's a good one. Listen here to me, me good man, listen here to me avic—I would want to be richer nor the Aga Khan to buy them things. *Them's the dearest cigarettes you could buy!* You take ten ordinary fags and weigh them against *twenty* of these lads and you'll find the ten fags is heavier. Cheap? Ho-ho, that's a good wan—and you a B. Comm. an' all. Have you no sense, man?'

Latin Corner

Crus-Keen Lawn

AMPHORA PLENA
Melii Equulei
DE CRURE FRACTO
Dissertatio

AH! HEU, EHEU! hei mihi misero! Jam quiescit leo furiosus, jam aquila impavida saxoso in domo se somno dat, jam infirmata est felis et jam—O eheu!—jam ludunt mures ridiculosi, hi Patriae mures qui apud me tam saepenumero tremuerunt!

> Sicut fortis equus, spatio qui saepe supremo
> Vicit Olympia, nunc senio confectus quiescit.

Sicut ipsa Hibernia, vester submissus servus est in duas partes divisus et in dolore diem ac noctem vivit, positus in lecto doloroso, eheu! Quid dicam? *Quid faciam?*

Mehercule nescio. Tempus est medecinae sed—hei!—celeriter non tempus fugit nec labuntur anni. Cum in me C.I.E. impetum fecerunt, tunc dolui, itaque ego nunc doleo; pedes, oculos, caput, latera, pulmones doleo, tristes sunt horae meae. Quid faciam iterum interrogo? Nihil. 'Quid est enim aliud Gigantum modo bellare cum dis nisi naturae repugnare.' Sed semper doleo. (Praeter Persicos apparatus et profanum vulgus) odi celebritatem, fugio homines, lucem adspicere vix possum.

Franguntur tibia fibulaque, sed sum nondum finitus, nec per cretam longam. Accidere episcopo potuisset. Discite, lectores carissimi, ex atra sorte mea—

Hodie mihi

Cras tibia!

Sarsfield, ut Graeci aiunt, *estin ho logos, kai Sarsfield estin ho anthropos.* De me, mutatis mutandis, fabula narratur. Est canis senex ad viam arduam. Caveat igitur stultus quisque sceleratus, caveat hic qui ad gloriam reipublicae laborare simulat, caveant Curiae oratores inanes, caveant nocentes fori nigri, caveant epistolarum ad *Tempora Gadelica* scriptores, caveant omnes qui de artis natura fulminant, et C.I.E. —caveantissimant! Et *maidir len a bhfuil againn de Ghaoilibh anois i nEirinn beo (—ní admhûm go bhfuil Eire beo!)* dóibh-sin *is molta an tost a mheastar thar seoda, an* silentia aurea *a chôoireann do'n bhfáinne óir.* Si nunc scribere non bene possim ac dicta factave aliorum in pejorem partem trahere, audire et legere possum et omnia semper in animo fixa habeo.

Aliquando Cicero de senectute disputationem fecit sed— mihi videtur—convenientius de crure fracto meo scribere potuisset, ut infra sit manifestum, verbis ('crus fractus' et 'senectus') mutandis:

Etenim, cum complector animo, quattuor reperio causas cur crus fractus miser videatur, unam, quod avocet a rebus gerendis, alteram, quod corpus faciat infirmius. [Ho-ho-ho!—M. na gC.] tertiam, quod privet fere omnibus voluptatibus [Hmmmm—M. na gC.] quartam, quod haud procul absit morte [Phew!—M. na gC.].

A rebus gerendis, dicet Cicero, crus fractus abstrahit? Quibus? Nihil ergo agebat Q. Maximus, nihil L. Paulus? Ceteri cruribus fractis, cum rem publicam consilio et auctoritate defendebant, nihil agebant? Non viribus aut velocitate aut celeritate corporum res magnae geruntur sed consilio, auctoritate, sententia.

De altera causa—'quod crus fractus corpus faciat infirmius'—Cicero ad hunc modum loquitur: quattuor robustos filios, quinque filias, tantam domum, tantas clientalas Appius regebat et caecus et crusfractus; intentum enim animum tanquam arcum habebat nec languescens succumbebat crure fracto; tenebat non modo auctoritatem, sed etiam imperium in suos, metuebant servi, verebantur liberi, carum omnes habebant; vigebat in illa domo patrius mos et disciplina . . .

Et de 'voluptatibus'?

Sequitur tertia vituperatio cruris fracti dicit Cicero, quod eam carere dicunt voluptatibus. *O praeclarum munus cruris*

*fracti, siquidem id aufert a nobis quod est in adulescentia vitiosis-
simum!* Nullam capitaliorem pestem quam voluptatem cor-
poris . . . Hinc patriae proditiones, hinc rerum publicarum
eversiones, hinc cum hostibus clandestina colloquia nasci,
nullum denique scelus, nullum malum facinus esse, ad quod
suscipiendum non libido voluptatis impelleret . . .! Quia non
modo vituperatio nulla, sed etiam summa laus cruris fracti
est quod ea voluptates nullas magnopere desiderat!

Et Cicero de morte?

Quarta restat causa . . . adpropinquatio mortis, quae certe
a crure fracto non potest esse longe. O miserum vir cruris
fracti, qui mortem contemnendum esse non viderit! O praeclarum diem, cum in illud divinum animorum concilium
coetumque profiscar cumque ex hac turba conluvione
discedam.

Ah well, hic ego jaceo in valetudinarium hospitio Dublin-
ensi; est mihi 'crus in urbe', ab oculis meis occultatis sub
tabernaculo albo; et cum Horatio cano:

O crus, O quando ego te adspiciam!

Vale!

(Nota Pedis: Cicero 'de Senectute' hoc modo de me scrip-
sit: *Olympiae per stadium ingressus esse Milo dicitur, cum
humeris sustineret bovem.*

Reipsa, animal masculus fuit, et hic fecit Cicero taurum
hibernicum!

Iterum vale!)

You remember that some time ago Dunsany—*vana fiducia
elatus*—tried his hand at translating an ode of Horace and
rashly put the result in the *Bell*? Well, I had to condemn the
whole business at the time, of course, it doesn't do to have
people going about interfering in my affairs. Last night I
translated all the Satires into Italian, much more ticklish
business than you'd imagine, considering the congruity of the
media. Ever try horsewhipping a horse? You get the point?
It *seems* easy, natural, obvious—but it's nearly impossible. I
append hereto a translation, very much free-style, I fear, of
one of these translations, and beg to be understood to say that
it is a wholly delightful and masterly rendering of the poem
in which Horace states his needs.

Please give me, Lord, it's all I ask,
A fairly large-size brandy cask,
With brazen hoops about its girth
In case its belly burst from mirth,
And in this tree a tiny tap
To measure out the golden sap.
Not quick or profligately at all
But by the half-one or the ball
And please arrange to have it set
In some underelict maisonette,
The sort of place which if you please
Would cost six thousand without fees,
Located nearly anywhere
But Merrion or Fitzwilliam Square,
And preferably where I can dress
For night shows at the R.D.S.
Without the need for forking out
A dollar to a taxi lout.
Please also have the house contain
A wife of twenty and a wain,
Two servant girls from Swanlinbar,
A nurse, a gardener and a char,
And furniture to indicate
There's people there (or were of late),
And flowers and pictures placed with care.
('What faultless taste!'—when I'm not there!)
Mementoes also please provide,
In shape of tusk or rug or hide
To show a caller that my aim
Was formerly at biggish game.
Ferocious beasts whose lairs have been
Tropical, polar and marine.
A sport that called for skill and luck
And practically unbounded pluck.
I want to have as well as those
Incredibly expensive clothes,
Enormous jewels (not of paste)—
A hint at my Byzantine taste—
And naturally it's understood
No man in my position could
Afford to loll inside the back
Of lesser car than Cadillac.
One other point I'd like made clear—
It's not my wish that I appear

Just muscular and wealthy, far
From interested in *objets d'art*,
Or thinking that a Bach Chorale
Is used for horses, that Pascal
Grew pansies or that James Joyce bases
His fame on *Irish Names of Places*—
Remembering naught of letters save
That Gorgon Zola wrote *Le Rêve*.
I'd rather be, if you don't mind,
A man of quite another kind:
Let not the cups I won for golf
Exclude a love of Hugo Wolff,
Picasso can be reconciled
With hunting lions in the wild;
I do not feel my war with leo
Unfits me for the Archduke Trio
Or that, if I'm grown rich and fat,
I can't read Proust because of that.
I only ask to be allowed
To stand out brightly from the crowd,
Be famous, and have critics say
That I'm the sun that lit my day—
Though knowing well that never could
My genius be quite understood
And when I die, please raise no stone—
Just have me done by Joseph Hone.

Great excitement was caused yesterday at Rineanna by the strange behaviour of an enormous Skymaster with zebra markings, suspected to have been stolen from the hangars of Hiberno-American Air-Lions Incorporated and piloted by a relative of the Corporation's President, Sir Myles na gCopaleen (the da). The machine, coming in from the sea, made several manoeuvres resembling bomb runs over the airport, causing the staff to take cover. Directions to land were ignored and all signals received were in Latin. The first exchanges are understood to have been as follows:

CONTROL: *Rineanna calling Skymaster Zebra. Come in on the beam, Skymaster. Over.*

SKYMASTER: Ohe, Frenator! Plus!

CONTROL: *Come in on the beam, Skymaster!*

SKYMASTER: Receptio mala, linguaque vestra ab intelligentia sensuque disjuncta! iterum!

CONTROL: *Skymaster, keep air-speed! Come in on the beam, Skymaster!*

SKYMASTER: Prorsum nihil intelligo!

CONTROL: *Skymaster,* accipite directionem ab radio!

SKYMASTER: *Radio Eireann?*

CONTROL: *You are too low, Skymaster—do not try to land!* Discedite! Abite! Quis es? Quo et unde?

SKYMASTER: Quis? Viatores honesti! Loquimur C. Pontii Romani ritu: 'Justus est coelidominus, Frenatores, quibus necessaria et pia Rineanna, quibus nulla nisi in Rineanna reliquitur spes. Oleum nostrum rarescet!' Audite Ovidium Nasonem: 'Pacis et armorum superis imisque deorum, Arbiter, alato qui pede carpet iter.' Muryaa, mehercule! 'Alato qui pede *carpet* iter!' Est coelidominus 'carpet magicus'? Ubi, ubi terrarum summus? Ubi haec Rineanna? Civitates Conjunctae?

CONTROL: *Consider crash-land in sea, Skymaster!* Cave, cave, coelidomine! Cave, oleum vestrum est rarum!

SKYMASTER: Oleum quod rarescit est vitae aqua, stulte! Audite Horatium:

> Non usitata non tenui ferar
> Penna, biformis per liquidum aethera
> Vates; neque in terris morabor
> Longius; invidiaque major
> Urbes relinquam. *Ubi sumus?*

CONTROL: Prope ad terram, ultra quain salis est.

SKYMASTER: Sed ubinam?

CONTROL: Terram Hiberniae Reipublicae.

SKYMASTER: Hercule! Sumus in hemisphaerio pravo! Erat iter nostrum tenebricosum ad ... ad aercampum Anseris Masculi!

CONTROL (*aside*): *Your man is elephants, he thought he was over Gander!* Cave, *Skymaster!*

SKYMASTER: Eheu, Hibernia! Tempus fugit! Nomen hujus coelidomini est *Tempus!* Vale!

After this extraordinary exchange, the gigantic aircraft disappeared oceanwards but re-appeared over the airport shortly afterwards, dropped several flares in broad daylight and started sending out morse signals in Latin seeking a radium *from 'Anser Masculus'. A drunken voice was then heard remarking that 'there was no answer'. After circling several times, the aircraft disappeared in the direction of Cork.*

(NOTE: *A Skymaster aircraft* Tempus *is registered as the flagship of the new corporation, American Super-Cloud Transport, and has been expected for some days on a survey flight. The title of this concern is shortly to be altered to Pan-Inter-Air Incorporated, and it is expected to operate Irish emigrant services.*

Up to a late hour last night Gárdaí in a Tiger Moth were investigating the mysterious occurrence.)

Requiem Writings

Professor Binchy's appreciation of Osborn Bergin in Saturday's paper was well said. Bergin was, surely, the scholar of the world. His death closes a formidable page in this country's record of profound and abstract learning. Bergin's passing should be mourned all the more for a reason said by another memorably unique person—*mar ná beidh a leithéid arís ann*. You do not find this dedicated type growing up today. Bergin found it necessary to learn at least six languages thoroughly in order to carry out his probes into Early and Middle Irish. Some of your scholars of today speak even English with difficulty, and very few (myself excluded) have penetrated to the heart of this thing euphemistically called 'the Irish language'. Having reached this focus of philological Antarctica, we have found ourselves inarticulate, gagged. We cannot communicate our discoveries. To some extent, I personally over-reached Bergin in my day. For one small poem which he wrote in old Irish, a pre-Christian tongue, on the subject of Mary having a little lamb, I wrote and published several discourses in Middle Irish. For some reason, in considering the death of a great man like Bergin, I cannot exclude from my mind a grand wee North of Ireland man who not only writes Irish at every available opportunity, but also undertakes to teach it to adults. Discussing books recently he talked about the scarcity of people *le iad a leamh*. You see?

It is no irreverence, I hope, to say that Bergin, in addition to being a true scholar, was also a character. Unperceptive people might have called him a crank. On the most formal occasions, when other persons in faultless evening dress wore mysterious 'orders', Bergin turned up in tweed knickerbockers. As a lecturer he was unique. Half-said words got lost in his beard; he began his lecture coming into the hall (the door of which he usually forgot to close), and he sometimes walked out in mid-sentence. Nobody knew even what language he was talking. On one occasion he lost his way in the university corridors, and lectured a class of veterinary students who expected to be informed on the merits of certain cattle drenches. And so they were, they concluded, for nobody could prove the contrary.

When Father Peter O'Leary was being buried, it is recorded that Bergin kept gazing disconsolately into the grave after the coffin had been lowered. Kind friends eventually guided him aside, knowing how wounded he was by the death of his old friend. They counselled fortitude and prayer in that evil hour.

'It's not that,' Bergin said. 'There were five elementary mistakes on the breast-plate.'

Bergin was, as Professor Binchy has recorded, a very shy man. And so he was. But he was often to be seen of an evening above in Rathgar, in Con Curran's house, playing the fiddle. He rested the instrument on his knee, shanachie-wise, and sawed away for further orders. It was usually a muttered tune, like his own speech. Still, it revealed the man.

He will be mourned by many, but particularly by the JugendHerrBergin.

Gogarty

There is a phrase, normally used ironically, that there is very few of them left. I hope it is permissible for myself to record here, in a corner often used for derision, a personal but also very widespread regret at the passing of Oliver St John Gogarty. Requiem-writing (if I may invent that phrase) is difficult, and could easily be presumptuous or even offensive, no matter much what the intention. But I personally knew this great man and here attempt to record qualities known also to the many others who knew him.

He had courage.

This word is usually ascribed as the attribute of an Irishman. Sometimes some diminishing qualification is added, such as 'physical'. It implies, and often is intended to do so, an absence of other forms of courage. Confining this remark of mine to Gogarty's own respect for the dignity of language, I would be content to say merely that he had courage. That quality, almost obsolete, does not need an adjective. When one says that somebody was good, one derogates rather than adds when one says he was 'very good'.

Courage is never enough. One trouble about it is that its possessor is hardly ever out of trouble and requires other skills for self-extraction. That last word is not to be confused with self-exculpation, but if a man wishes to be elsewhere (possibly on a professional medical appointment) and is talking to a friend (the late Alf Bergan, for instance), he does not make a crude or objectionable exit.

Two minutes of that tongue and very subtle mind at the back would convince anybody of his day that Gogarty's departure involved for the party of the other part something of the nature of a bereavement. To a stranger it may seem that he was glib. Less glib or more honest man I personally never met. Wit, adjustment to an existing situation, improvisation, all those qualities he had, he had in a profusion unexampled. Now and again a remark seemed cruel. Occasionally a handy quotation betrayed him into saying something that seemed unkind. Against whom can this charge not be laid? Even his majesty the sun has spots.

Was Gogarty afraid to die? A curiosity about him—perhaps of a rather literary kind—is the number of times he considered this emergency in verse. He was, after the manner of his day, addicted to classical mode. He discerned much of merit in the work of Catullus. Familiar though it be, let this be his epitaph:

> Enough! Why should a man bemoan
> A Fate that leads the natural way?
> Or think himself a worthier one
> Than those who braved it in their day.
> If only gladiators died,
> Or heroes, Death will be his pride;
> But have not little maidens gone,
> And Lesbia's sparrow—all alone?

The restatement thus of an ancient thought ennobles the man who did it. I think that is true. But may Gogarty himself forgive if this morning I feel sentimental. The fact is that I am.

Criticism

Due to some blunder, some leakage, some monstrous breach of faith—I accuse nobody, mind!—a statement, a *pronunciamento*, from that sturdy mountain republic, Mr G. Bernard Shaw, has been released in London without the customary simultaneous endorsement from my office. There will be no inquiry this time—I detest fuss!—but this is as good a time as any for setting the record straight. Do I agree with Mr Shaw or not? I agree, of course; Mr Shaw and I are old men—there is nothing really that we can quarrel about. Whom, indeed, could either of us hope to convince? Mr S.'s fancy this time is that old selling-plater, Euthanasia, (ch. f. by Muddleshead—Nervous Dyspepsia, 2,000 yrs); he thinks hanging is taking your capital punishment the hard way. True, and think of all the people you know that hanging is too good for them. I'm an expert on this—my capital knows more about punishment than you'd think; considering I've been living on it since I left Maynooth. Mr Shaw says that

... the present restriction of liquidation to murder cases, and the exemption of dangerous lunatics (who should be liquidated as such, crime or no crime), will cease, and must be replaced by State-contrived euthanasia for all idiots and intolerable nuisances, not punitively, but as a necessary stroke of social economy ...

Obviously, but I should like to hear more of this 'present restriction'—surely it is not to be assumed that contemporary defensive crusades on a neighbouring continent can be collectively stigmatised as ... 'murder cases'? Surely the liquidation of certain towns—far too old anyway—cannot be regarded otherwise than as a sort of ... ethnic euthanasia? Or can it be that when Mr Shaw talks of 'liquidation' and 'murder cases' he has in mind merely current practice in the licensed trade? It is good to know that the exemption of dangerous lunatics will soon cease: I had often wondered about that and, though of course I am awfully sorry about it, I can't help being just a little relieved to hear that 'intolerable nuisances' at least aren't going to live here any more. Of course that still leaves us with the ordinary common-or-garden nuisances. Can't be helped I suppose: we must be thankful for small Mausers. There's just one little point though that—speaking as a former trans-Alpine pro-consul—I don't quite get. Who ... who will nominate the ... em ... the intolerable nuisances and the dangerous lunatics? Will you do the thing on a vocational basis? Or would you open it up to universal franchise? Would unsuccessful candidates in some cases have to ... forfeit their deposits? Have you considered the piteous condition of persons who commit crimes (rather than virtues) not being dangerous lunatics; will they be ineligible for a siesta in the gas chamber?

One small doubt. Has a clear case been made that this euthanasia should be *State-contrived*? Is it properly a central charge? Would the cost be more appropriately borne on the rates? I rather think so. For this country, at all events, I would prefer to see County Council euthanasia: for indeed do not the ratepayers bear at present—and so unfairly—the burden of maintaining idiots and lunatics—and in luxurious surroundings?

Yes, it is a fine scheme and far more attractive to a man of my age than any plan which takes as its basic assumption that intolerably vulgar superstition, pananthropic insurance. It interests me too for another reason: if you can now determine not merely who is worthy of death but when he may die, I take it that you understand exactly what is implied by ... life? I take it that you have fully calculated the prophylactic qualities of death? These idiots, these nuisances, these poor types—are you sending them on ... before you? Or are you not going ... my way? (Sighs, removes biretta, and falls asleep.)

The Editor of the Grammar School of Drogheda, County Lout, has written two letters to the Headmaster of this newspaper, eliciting one reply from our admirable Minister for Education Commission, the Hon. Horace Plunkett. First to last, the entire correspondence was destitute of that uranial tabernacle of authority, my imprimatom, and thus partakes of the substance of treason, naked and terrible. I stigmatise the thing here and now as juvenile delinquency and will deal personally with the ringleaders at no far distant date.

There is this, however, about crime—it has for the scientific observer its quantum of illumination over that dark bourne so long my especial focus of study, the insatiable vessel of my immense pity and holy patience—the world of men. What then is revealed by this sceleric manifestation at Drogheda? Nothing less, my masters, than this—that the authorities of the Drogheda Grammar School *appear to be completely misled as to the function of education*! All learning, all purported indoctrination of juveniles, all schooling were clearly folly, were vanity, were sinful arrogation of pride— unless directed to the legitimate end—the comprehension of my daily discourses. Upon this basis it will be seen that the propositions of the head of the school, Mr Fleming Thompson (I substitute no 'a' in Fleming) instantly fall to the ground.

'Realising the burden imposed on the boy,' Mr Thompson says, 'in studying English, Latin, French and Irish, in addition to the mother tongue Danish, I asked the Department . . . to bring such pupils under a rule giving exemption from Irish.'

A number of astounding propositions here emerge. First, that the study of languages is 'a burden'. (Forsooth is learning also a burden?) Second, that, if a boy is required to learn five languages, English, French and Danish should be included. *But I do not write in Danish*—and I thought that *everybody*, even Danish boys born in England, already knew English and French, else how do they expect to prosper in business enterprises?

'We would, of course, eliminate Latin,' Mr Thompson says. 'We are not, however, prepared to sacrifice any pupils on the altar of compulsory Irish.'

Quite. But I *thought* that the sole function of Latin—apart from its occasional inclusion in my discourses—was to enable the educated classes to come to an elucidation of the knottier points in the syntax of the Greek authors, since the footnotes in all proper editions of such work are always in Latin. *Yet Greek is nowhere mentioned in Mr Thompson's correspondence!* And whence comes this incompatibility as between Latin and

Irish? Irish *is* Latin—surely I explained that before—Latin improved by occidental vernacularity, *and* let me point out, of what nature is this 'altar' of comb pull (sorry!) Irish? The word is *Latin*, which proves my argument.

'While the Department may now allow a language such as Danish,' Mr Thompson says (recklessly, I hold), 'I cannot see them ever agreeing to that language replacing Irish.'

And fwy not? There is no limit to what the Department might do, but please note this: Danish once replaced Irish, in Drogheda as well as in Dublin; again Irish replaced Danish. Could not Danish again replace Irish?

No. Leaving aside the primary purpose of languages as a means of the study of my own immense pieties: the profane purpose of education is the liberation of the mind from all cants, superstitions, shibboleths and unclean political creeds. There can thus be no such thing as an educational establishment which is *in any sense* partisan in matters of mundane folly.

And, I know of only four languages, viz: Latin, Irish, Greek and Chinese. These are languages because they are the instruments of integral civilisations. English and French are not languages: they are mercantile codes.

On behalf of the Medical Profession, where I am highly and constantly o'steamed and where my degree of M.W.D. (W for 'witch') carries great weight (consisting of ball, chain, bells, iron mask, cast-iron rattle, steel mace)—you ought to see my weighing rooms!—I solemnly and formally reject and abjure statements attributed by a daily newspaper some little time ago to a gentleman writing in the *Journal of the Medical Association of Eire*. (M.A.E.?)

The article in question (if it existed at all) was not unfraught with information concerning odd epistemological epiphenomena—e.g., invariably posterior location of principles, necessity for the employment of wide gauge in establishing principles, essential dependence of scientific horticulture on retrospective movement vis-à-vis principles specified above, identity of total process outlined above with that involved in the employment of trees as optical aids in the examination of sylvan developments, both processes to be recognised as a solution to the 'real problem of education'. Ha——ho—— let me quote:

The real problem of education was to make the pupil see the wood by means of the trees. In other words, detailed knowledge was absolutely necessary, but was only fruitful if the teacher kept constantly referring back to broad principles.

There is more and we may as well get through with it because I want to bring in a verdict before the conclusion of this . . . address. The young author, referring to the present system of education, writes:

. . . that it is an honest enough system, but a dull one, a system which believed in the overriding importance of the examination and of factual information . . .

(Deadly silence.) I . . . I . . . see . . . No more exams, eh? Just take it on a fellow's word, I mean gentlemen simply don't tell lies? *You a doctor, old man? Of course, old boy— in a way I'm an M.D., you know.* I see. And no more factual information? That's a very good one indeed—might I be permitted to inquire just exactly what . . . alternative—information is envisaged as an improvement? Eh? Would . . . lies be a help? But I interrupt.

The student spent long hours learning Irish, which he probably would never use unless he wanted to get a job, so that a spirit of cynicism was early inculcated . . .

A moment please—am I to take it that M.A.E. thinks it's rather caddish to . . . want a job? Hah? That it's a cynical ungentlemanly act and that a normal fellow would be far better off living off the father's meagre salary as sub-temporary clinical psychopathic inspector grade III, un-estd.? Ah well, so long as we know, so long as we have some . . . inkling of what the younger generation has in its mind, fair enough. We don't mind getting up early in the morning to go in and sign the booooook. Please heaven we'll be retiring next year though—and sure plaze God we'll all be quite comfortable together on the grand little wan hundhred a year pinshin. Ah, yes . . .

But here, make way for the dull grind and God be with the old-fashioned brilliant grind.

When the dull grind had gone on for five or six years of adolescence, without any attempt to encourage the pupils to apply his hard-earned knowledge to life, was it any wonder that the unfortunate young product of this coldly unimaginative system arrived at the university quite firmly convinced that work was never interesting . . .

Musha, musha, then, and was it? But whence this assurance that adolescence lasts only five or six years?

I do not read or write books now—much. I gave that game up—and as a young man I did the same when a disgruntled and underpaid dipper of arthritic colonels at Bad Nauheim—as a Bad Job. The game isn't worth the three candles and O'Loughlin will tell you the same. But I do read 'reviews'. They permit one to view contemporary literary eructations through a glass darkly, though rarely is it done darkly enough. Here is something I seen in the paper recently. (Why *the* paper? Is there, then, another?)

But everywhere one can discern the master's hand—in the construction, in the racy narrative, in the rich spit-natural dialect, in the lightning delineation of appearance and personality:
'He had a red face, an apoplectic face, that looked like a plum pudding you'd squeezed up and down till it all bulged sideways, so that the features were all flattened and spread out and the two eyes narrowed into slits . . .'

That extract, with quotation inset, is from a notice dealing with a book of short stories by Mr Frank O'Connor. Mr O'Connor and I are old friends, though heavens knows of whom, and I yield to nuns in my admiration for his work—if not for his literary work. But if he wrote that bit about the plum pudding—and melaw we are not admitting that he did —then I, in my capacity as an old and trusted *chef de l'état major de cuisine*, must . . . must really protest. If this be so, and I still doubt it, I can only ask Mr O'Connor to come along down to the club some evening, black tie, bring a few friends, and also bring a mangle, steam press, or whatever other instrument he may choose for the experiment. I shall put up the plum pudding—no charge to guests of the nation —and it only remains for him to go to work, the results to be published in one evening two morning papers.

Gentle reader, have you ever squeezed a plum pudding *up* and down? What is the strength of a plum pudding in compression and tension? What is its modulus of elasticity, where its extensible limit, in what elevated thermic stratum its flash point? Who will attempt to deny that even the worst plum puddings fracture at something under 1·05 oz per superficial year? Fracture, mark you, crumble and lose all integrity! I have had Purcell test more plum puddings in my day than any other man in these islands; he will tell you the same thing —test them at seven days, test them at twenty-eight, their strength—be the fault in mixing or in aggregate—declines as they mature!

There is one other matter. It is this question of the 'features' and the 'two [*sic*] eyes'. Hmmmmmmmmmm. Strong drink I have never permitted to pass these lips—true there is always a bottle of Hennessy in the house but that is in case the missus should have a seizure (blast those rate collectors!), but this much I can say with my hand upon my heart; never, never have I seen a plum pudding with features, never a pudding with even one eye. Never never never. There was one Christmas, I admit, but something . . . someone . . . I don't know, but that cider cup was . . . ah, well. The best of us have our lapses and human nature is human nature.

I am, of course, terribly interested in our younger writers and if they be from Cork, then my warm understanding of their problems is boundless, my sympathy immense. I may well be mistaken in the mild strictures I have felt bound to make above. I add with candour that I have never seen a Cork plum pudding. For all I know it may be a very different thing from the dun confection that is known to me. The Cork plum pudding may wear a hat and go to Limerick Junction races.

There is one matter which the three B's—Bevin, Byrnes and Bidault—appear to ignore . . . (incidentally how many Bs were there in my Bonnet?). There is one most grave and vital thing which—Heaven forgive me if I wrong them!—they appear to have forgotten. There is one most powerful and dreadful element which they have reckoned without and it is my unofficial view that this lack of animadvertence may yet prove their undoing. I am speaking, as the bored reader will be quick to recognise, of my patients (stet) and I am desired to state that is by no means inexhaustible. Molotov is doing his best. He is my friend, and he has the interests of his country at Czprtqdt (pron. 'harrt') (in the Crimea) and I, who, in a way, am a true Irishman, will not stand by while the hirelings of the plutocratic cryptocrats jeer at him for his simplicity. M. Bevin, Britain's distinguished White Russian agent, should know better than to expose to the scorn of the light-headed public the foibles of a man who is, it seems to me, a saint, and the Editor of the South Irish Tombs, that anonymous and probably villainous nocturnalist, mark, I pray you, how he pranceth and yelpeth on the side of the big battalions to the everlasting disgrace and burning resentment of his specious (stet) correspondent M. na gCopaleen, member of Mr McBride's Shadow Cabinet! Alas that these mine eyes should ever, being opened, have encountered, within the decent folds of a family newspaper, these words if words indeed they be:

. . . all the nations want peace as soon as possible, and if the truth were known, Russia probably wants it more quickly than anyone else. Why then is Mr Molotov so consistently obstinate? Why will he agree to nothing? Why does he seem to go out of his way to hamper his colleagues' efforts to make at least a start with the conclusion of peace? The sad truth seems to be that the Russians trust nobody. Their attitude during the war was entirely cynical . . .

Starting backwards, naturally, I have the honour to ask for a definition of cynicism. Fowler, who should know better, says that a cynic is 'a philosopher of sect founded by Antisthenes, marked by ostentatious contempt for pleasure'. Is that, pray, a bad thing in a world driving footlong to destruction on a road lined with 'seven-day' 'hotels', S.P. shops, and cinemas wherein love, friendship and the family are degraded and brought into contempt by irreverent showmen who misprise eternity and vainly seek a spurious happiness in the accumulation of specie, bullion and most legal tender? Is it then wrong when war threatens the homeland to exchange the toys and baubles of effeminate civilisation for the broadsword of valour and self-sacrifice? Is it . . . unBritish? And

... 'to trust nobody'!!!!! O strange reproach on thinnest
Irish lips. For, let us take the thing at its lowest level, *whom*
... *whom*, ladies and gentlemen, *does* the Editor of the *Irish
Times* trust when he doesn't trust me ... with more than six
pennies per week tram-money!!! (O ignoble stipend! O
small soul! O narrow unfriendly spirit and alas for the old-
fashioned Ship Money!)

Pay, I implore, dear readers, no whit of attention to the
maddened dithyrambs of this distinguished but unscrupulous
journalist, this wisecap editor who asks without shadow of
smile 'why Mr Molotov is so consistently obstinate' (forsooth!); 'why he will agree to nothing' (I' faith!). Precisely
whose fool does the Editor conceive Mr Molotov to be? Not
Jimmy's, certainly; not that of Georges (How crazy
'Georges's' would look!);—nay, not even Ernst von Bevin
can best this clever Oriental de Valera! And must we pretend
that Mr Molotov is ... unwise to distrust the ... the wet,
stern, demi-cracies (stet), traditional friends and patrons of
the Bolshevist way of life? A nice fool Mr M. would look if
he were *not* obstinate—three guesses whose Little Father
would be back in the Winter Palace before you could say Jack
Robins, Hun, complete with terribly interesting diary and
ecclesiastical friend with beard? Hah? Does anyone think
that *I'd* agree to anything if I were in Mr M.'s place? Not on
your suuite, '*Life!*'

Right there in the very heart of France, surrounded by
pious Frenchmen whose sole (and unique) aim it is to crush
bit by bit every bit of decent feeling, family life, jokes, etc.,
right off the face of the earth by means of manly poems
('. . . *mais, O mon coeur, entends le chant des matelots* . . .').
Grown-up paintings and terribly strong. I mean, existentialist
novels dealing with life, and the insulting absurdity of it all
don't you think? Would I agree to anything, *anyway*? No.
That mush (stet) at least is certain. But I wd. say to the lad
Malley-Taaffe, I wd. say: Keep your eye on Bidault, Remember Moscow and oppose everything *n'importe quoi*. (I
was the very same myself when I came up here to Dublin
first, a tremulous, old-fashioned boy, who imagined that very
long ladders must be needed to reach even the first floor lofts
in the Merrion Square houses! I trusted no one. I even

refused to tell a policeman the time. Thought it was a trick to
see had I the grandfather's gold watch. Thought he probably
wasn't a real policeman—thought he just hired the suit for
the day, and was really after my watch. Thought I knew a
trick worth two of that. Did. Went into a shop, asked for a
suit of plain clothes. Fellow said I can give them to you all
right, but . . . I feel it would be a pity to spoil you. What do
you mean, I said. Well, he said, those silver buckles in your
shoes, he said, old boy, he said they *alone*, and he said I am
not taking into account that very fine Taal coat, your *hata
Charoilin and* the worsted stockings, old man, he said, I could
allow you five shillings on them sho-es! It was, need I say, a
bargain . . .)

But how *clever* of Ed. *I.T.* to have spotted this:

'All the nations want peace as soon as possible . . .' By
heavens, let no one try to fool the old man, he knows what
he's doing I can tell *you*!

In expensive restaurants it is customary to include in the
printed bill of fare a number of *recherché* dishes so costly that
there is practically no chance that anybody will order them.
They give the menu an opulent and exclusive look, and
ordinary customers who come in for steaks are grateful that
they are permitted to eat them in surroundings apparently
frequented by millionaires. Should some person, being
drunk, ask for one of these dishes, the waiter can always
apologise and say it is 'off'—thus suggesting an inundation of
millionaires earlier in the day and thus making the dismal
restaurant appear even more snooty. Mind you, I do a bit of
that sort of thing myself an odd time, out in the house in
Santry. 'Anybody like a glass of Polish vodka?' I sometimes
ask my guests, exhibiting an unlabelled bottle of colourless
fluid. (It is four parts potheen, one part Burmese rice gin.)
They pretend to consider, then decline, saying a drop of
Irish would suit them if there was such a thing in the house.
There isn't but they still get it. (The prescription is parts 2
sherry wine, parts 2 Scotch and parts 3 turps.) They drink it
and say nothing. (Perhaps they can't speak.) Still, I am convinced that there is nothing gained in this country by putting
correct labels on bottles. Probably that's why publicans don't

do it. Nor do people who call other things by their correct names fare any better.

Let's change the subject and talk about Radio Eireann. Do you known, lads, I think Brennan is going to do a first-class job there. (On the new short-wave station, I mean—Radio Eireann itself is perfect.) And why wouldn't he? Hasn't he a grand staff, and now Larry Morrow and Francis MacManus in on top of them? (Though I wouldn't take that last man's job for anything—he'll have such a pile of manuscripts on his desk every morning that he'll begin to wonder whether his name is Francis MacManuscripts!)

But . . .

I'll tell you a funny thing about the Americans. They're terribly terse and simple, particularly when announcing their radio programmes in the newspapers. Perhaps they think that most people can read only words of one syllable, but this is usually what they give the newspapers to cover an hour and a half of A.F.N. broadcasting time:

> News
> Talk
> Discs

In a way, perhaps it tells you about as much as you care to know. 'Discs' is a particularly honest sort of disclosure. They even have a special name for people who put the discs on the turn-table: they call them 'disc jockeys'. That's what they are, too.

What one loves about Radio Eireann is the romantic veils of Celtic embroidery with which the names of items are garnished. One reads this item, for instance

> From the Violin Repertoire
> Ida Haendel plays,

or

> Tuesday's Concert of Light
> Music: Mendelssohn and
> Schubert.

Sounds very nice, doesn't it. Costly, too—a distinguished violinist and a whole orchestra, all from little Radio Eireann.

An alternative method of advertising those two items would
be (respectively):

Discs

Discs

Please don't run away with the idea that everybody dis-
likes discs. Not at all—lots of people buy their own. It's not
the same thing though. You see, recordings made by good
artists would sound . . . funny if they were just played. It
wouldn't be a grown-up procedure, if you know what I
mean. Suppose you like Bing Crosby singing 'How Blue is
the Sky'. If you just buy it and play it, I fear you're rather a
brutish, simple sort of cove. The suave, adult and civilised
way of enjoying this song may be learned from the radio
presentation of it. The disc jockey speaks:

Well, here we are in the Manhattan Cocktail Bar. The place is
terribly crowded, famous people everywhere. Surely it isn't—yes,
it is!—over in the corner there in the middle of an admiring group
is Bing Crosby. My, I wonder would he sing for us if we asked
him nicely? Well, what can we lose by asking? I'll ring him on this
intertable telephone—thank you, waiter!—'Hullo! That you,
Bing? How about a song? What—you will? Good! What's it to
be? "How Blue is the Sky"? Good . . .'
(*Hiss of needle begins.*)

You see what I mean? For sheer *enjoyment*, I mean, for
grown-ups after the children have gone to bed, isn't that
absolutely grand? And how deceptive it would be if such a
programme were simply labelled 'Discs'.

Radio Eireann's other record ('Bless This House') is also
sometimes given a uniquely enjoyable setting that is, like
exquisite pastry on a pie, the best part of the whole thing.
Loquitur disc jockey, something like this:

I am now going to play that lovely recording 'Bless This
House' and the request is for 'Darkie' and 'Snowball' in Ward 4
of the Rotunda, from Mammie, Daddy, Rita, Marie-Louise,
Seamus, Thérèse, and all at Number 8 Sheebeen Terrace, hoping
that you will soon be well and convalescing at your Auntie
Maggie's in Youghal, who also sends her love; the request is also
for Nurse Susan Morphia in Cork Street Hospital from J.D., a
grateful patient; for Winston Churchill, whose birthday is today

and who is recovering from an operation in Charing Cross Hospital, from 'the Four Bright Sparks', also for M.A.C. in Mercers, from Mollie. (*Hiss of needle.*)

Before the war it was possible for cranks and perverts to go to bed, with cigarette alight and the glass of malt hard by, and listen to German stations broadcasting music for intervals of two and three hours, without a break to give the listener the pleasure of hearing the human voice, noblest of noises, giving out urbane and amusing chat about the music. Thank goodness that has been put a stop to. (By the way, why couldn't the gramophone companies record the disc jockeys' enthralling remarks on one side of a disc and the song on the other?) Last Sunday I listened to discs for two solid hours—music, three-quarters of an hour, chat, an hour and a quarter. Is this a record?

The language problem again—I *am* sorry but we must, you know. First, pronunciation; this is very important. Carelessness in the formation of vowels and consonants, when it is accompanied by improper breathing, bad phrasing and the forcing of the voice, leads inevitably to slovenly speech. Nothing produces so bad an impression on a stranger; you cannot give too much attention to this matter—with it is bound up the whole question of national prestige. Dublin people are perhaps the worst offenders in this respect. One thinks immediately of the words: 'Cow', 'Man', 'Office', 'Foreign', 'It', 'This', 'Carry', 'Dog', readers can finish the list (themselves). You know how they come out: 'Kehaouw', 'Mhaaanhh', 'Uffuss', 'Phurren', 'Ihh', 'Dis', 'Korry', 'Dawg' . . . It is simply not good enough, that is all. The language will never progress if we make no effort to speak it properly. Readers will appreciate that this is no mere academic problem. If the language is permitted to die the consequences will be terrible. 'No language, no Fatherland' says the old proverb and the present writer, who has lived for many years among zombies, believes that the situation may be even worse than the proverb would suggest. In the early days of the language movement we tended to think of it primarily as the sole badge of nationhood. It is that unquestionably, but the possibility of its disappearance raises even more uncomfortable issues. You see, mind you I'm no alarmist, but . . . some trading nations feel that any given nation should have . . . *some* language. If we fail to make the most of such little English as we now remember it may bode ill for us. These people, these trading tribes, may . . . stupidly . . . conclude that if we have no language it is possible that we are . . . not . . . people at all. There *are* still tribes old-fashioned enough to take the view that intelligible talk is one way by which one can distinguish humanity from the fauna, flora, etc. of this very beautiful world. (I can't, off hand, think of any other.)

True Story

A radio operator on the shores of one of our oceans had an interesting experience which I would like to relate to you. Up to recently, the messages he sent out were accurately received in distant continents by other operators of his own sex. It became necessary to replace these by girls. (The war.) The girls did their best but it happened that one of these technicians, in the course of doing her best, did not seem to be able to receive very well, not that there was anything wrong with the apparatus. The man at this end gradually became frantic; every minute he was being 'broken' with the request to *repeat that please*. Eventually he flashed out this: 'Do you EXPECT ME TO SWIM ACROSS WITH IT?'

Back, sure as fate, came the echo: 'REPEAT WORD AFTER SWIM . . .'

Heaven forbid that I should measure swords with Professor Einstein, even if both of us *are* qualified surveyors. (Besides, I happen to know the exact area: it is 1,034 acres 2 perches and pop. is 271 (normal), 1,631 (10.15 p.m.–midnight). Furthermore, it is still very cold (cf. *Hiberna*, winter quarters), though indeed if the job could be done at home with logs, there might be some point in it. (Probably decimal point.))

But I do not mind having a set 2 with Einstein and I will now probably quote the following words of the Professor, uttered *à propos* of the statement by Professor Schroedinger of the unified field theory in general mathematical terms. Declaring that the foundations of theoretical physics were not yet determined, Professor 1st! said:

The layman is naturally inclined to consider the course of development as such that the basis is obtained from the fact of experience by gradual generalisation and abstraction. This, however, is not the case. Rather one attempts to start from freely chosen conceptual elements and form them into a theoretical system in accordance with the principle of the greatest logical simplicity, and then examine this system for its usefulness for the explanation of the facts of experience. This examination is a task which presupposes the solution of difficult special mathematical problems. Professor Schroedinger's latest attempt must be considered as such an effort. It can, therefore, be judged only on the basis of its mathematical qualities, but not from the point of view of 'truth' and agreement with the facts of experience . . .

Do you know, I do not like that speech at all. First of all, note the assumption of the druidic mantle by the opening sneer, long, elaborate and utterly unworthy, directed at myself. I am, forsooth, a *layman*! And the layman is *naturally* inclined to consider something quite stupid. 'The layman is naturally inclined to consider that gold grows on trees. Such an idea is, however, at variance with the facts. Science has established that gold is a mineral . . .' That sort of thing. It is just abuse, nothing more. The Professor would do well to reflect that all men are laymen when dismounted from their individual hobby-horses. What does Einstein know of the use and meaning of words? Very little, I should say—though in that department of human folly he would no doubt, be 'inclined to consider' certain things in his capacity of layman. For instance, what does he mean by terms like 'truth' and 'the facts of experience'? We do not know and can therefore extract no meaning from his speech. His attempt to meet shrewd newspaper readers on their own ground is not impressive, and involves in his mind confusion of the function of the word and that of the mathematical symbol. Neither can be expressed in terms of the other. This is an absolute exclusion. No mathematical statement can be 'explained' in terms of words. The 'truth' and 'facts' established mathematically are mathematical truths and facts, things valid

within the mathematical canon but not necessarily reconcil-
able with either our Greek word *aletheia* or with that grim
corpus of hallucination, the 'facts of experience'. A straight
line produced to infinity is a mathematical truth. Outside
mathematics, it is an impossibility, an abstraction, a fancy, a
joke.

What, by the way, *are* these facts of experience with which
Einstein insists a proper system must square. What have we
of experience which is consistently and uniformly appre-
hended by humans and which can therefore be designated
'fact'?

I have certain duties as Assistant Secretary of the World,
not the least of which is—not 'teaching' (heaven forbid!)—
but rather the endless effort of trying to suggest to humans
the infinite immensity of their ignorance *and*—mark this!—
emphasising the danger and folly they wallow in when they
seek to illumine the tenebraical caverns of their own minds
with home-made torches. (Affected word 'tenebraical'?
Agreed.)

The following statements are statements of fact *ex
authoritatis natura*, having been made by me:

1 The 'science of theoretical physics' is not a science but a
department of speculation. Its speculative materials are
incomplete and fallacious: incomplete because elements
incapable of human observation are excluded: fallacious
because the limited observation possible is undertaken by
humans. Insofar as it purports to be concerned with investigating the causation of life according to rational criteria,
it is sinful.

2 Its procedure is the observation of what appear to be
natural 'laws' and the deduction therefrom of other 'laws' and
'facts'. A serious fallacy derives from this obsession with
order. All science is meaningless unless referable to the
human race. Physicists are deluded by the apparent orderli-
ness of the universe. They do not realise that the forces of
disorder—being energies residing in the human brain—are
immensely more powerful than those of order and are such as
to reduce planetary and other examples of order to inconse-
quence. The human mind is the paramount contemporary

mystery but it cannot be investigated as a preliminary to reform owing to the absence of extra-human investigators. With that mystery untouched, however, it is a futility to fiddle with the matters known as 'physics'. It is also manifest vanity.

3 All major 'scientific discoveries' do not add to what is already known but merely push farther back the horizon of human ignorance (i.e., the only sort of ignorance that exists): *Example:* Before the atom bomb existed researchers were addressing the finite and soluble problem of making the bomb. No other considerable problem existed in relation to the fission of nuclei. But the instant the bomb was made and used, there was created a limitless ignorance as to how a defence against the bomb could be devised. Thus the solution of ignorance A created the much greater ignorance B. There is an enormous net loss to Hugh Mannity. (These are very deep waters, of course.)

4 The term 'science of theoretical physics' is a contradiction. Einstein's terms 'truth' and 'facts of observation' have already been studied by hundreds of philosophers, and not to any agreed purpose. It is thus folly for physicists to isolate one little branch of terrestrial 'experience' and call the examination of it a science. No aspect of the world can be investigated or even observed without a simultaneous regard to the whole, and particularly to the gigantic abstractions known as thought, feeling, imagination, impulse. True and useful science must therefore be a synthesis of all the sciences, a thing that is generally called omniscience.

5 There are nearly six thousand National Schools in Eire. Even at this late day, is omniscience on the curriculum of a single one of them? Or—thanks to this mad policy of squandering time and money on the revival of Gaelic—are our young folk to leave school and go forth into the world completely unequipped for . . . death?

I fear my friend, Mr Sean O'Faoláin, will have to write less if he expects me to annotate *everything* he turns out. However . . . we will have a quick run through his latest discourse, which he entitles 'The Irish Colleen Is The Irish Coolie'. The title is all right, of course—it would be surprising to read that the Irish Colleen is the Japanese Coolie (heart-rending, also). (By the way, is there such a thing as an English Colleen?) Two foreign friends come to tea to Mr O'Faoláin. Know what they begin talking about? Come now, three guesses? (Ah no, you needn't try, it's only waste of time, you'd never guess.) *Literary censorship!* Bless my soul, I wish I had foreign friends who were such a divil for the books! (Or should I merely, and with more honesty, wish I had foreign friends?)

Before commenting on Mr O'Faoláin's friends, I must recount a most interesting experience I had in connection with this censorship question on Monday night last (no less). I am not one who willingly accepts cultural third-degree from the Third Programme but occasionally the programme is heard in our lovely home while we are standing by waiting for 'Listen In Larne' or, as on Monday, for a delightful poetry programme about Colmcille's shroud by Róibeárd O Faracháin entitled, if I remember aright, 'The First Textile'. Anyway, I found myself listening to a bit of this Third Programme on Monday: certain it is that I did not myself turn it on—probably it was one of the boys, Toirbhdhealbhach maybe, or possibly Fionnbhar or Mathghamhain. Do you know, I nearly passed out when I heard what was coming out of that radio. A 'play' dealing with A Certain Subject! I acted quickly, of course. The nine boys I sent out for a walk to Blanchardstown, the girls I despatched on a sham 'visit' to their granny's. (Herself? Ah no, I left *her* there, the mammy is in no danger from radios, believe you me. If any noise comes from it resembling music, she says 'Is that "Poet and Peasant"?'—naming the sole title of a musical piece known to her. If it is non-musical noise, even atmospherics she asks 'Is that the news?' Once, I need hardly say, it was the latter question she asked when the dread overture to 'Poet and Peasant' accidentally got in on the short waves. 'It is,' I answered wittily, 'and Bismarck is dead.' 'The poor man,' she said.

My point? What is the use of the Gaelic Government having expensive and elaborate machinery for censoring printed matter if a nearby radio transmitter can pour deluges of spoken filth into Irish ears, and on a wavelength which can be easily confused with that used by Radio Eireann? We can here learn from the wartime radio techniques. Ireland will be content with nothing less than a powerful jamming station, coupled with a three-clause Bill making listening to the Third Programme illegal! *And* we must take up the passports of Irish persons who would cross over to England to diffuse their nefarious 'stories' through this Third Programme. And if the jamming station should also jam Radio Eireann, it can't be helped. Human souls are the stake!

Now let us return to Mr O'Faoláin. His friends purported to 'criticise' our censorship. 'Let's skip it,' Mr O'Faoláin cries, 'it is a boring and humiliating subject and there is no explaining it away to an American, or a Swede, or a Frenchman.' I agree. Why should we be humiliated by these people? The cultural achievements of America and Sweden, formidable though they be, do not entitle them to quarrel with our standards of propriety. It is different perhaps in the case of France—it would be distressing to have the heroes of the Résistance think badly of us. (What must they think of the way we behaved after we had defeated the British? Not one effort was made to bring Mrs Churchill, Mrs Chamberlain, Lady Birkenhead or Mrs Lloyd George to trial!!!)

'Let us pass on,' says Mr O'Faoláin, 'to the subject of woman's place in Ireland.' And there, I regret, is where he and I go two ways. He tells of a very scandalous entertainment in which he took part with the two foreigners: they read through our Constitution—apparently with the object of mocking at it!! He quotes one passage:

In particular, the State recognises that by her life within the home woman gives to the State a support without which the common good cannot be achieved . . .

To me as to right-thinking citizens this is a reasonable piece of understatement. But Mr O'Faoláin's pals think differently.

They looked up from the page. 'It reminds one a little,' the wife said, 'of the Nazi idea of woman's place in the world—to be occupied with Cookery, Kids and the Kirk.' This woman was very troubled about the inferior position of women in Ireland.

The Nazis I do not know—if there was a family of that name in Dublin it was before my time but doubtless my poor father knew them. But I am very glad to know that the Nazis thought women should be interested in the Church. (It's quite sound, that. Children, also—science has established that children are best borne by women. It's an old-fashioned business, of course, but pretty efficient none the less.) Will I ever forget the night Finnbhfhlaitheartach came! I think Mr O'Faoláin's cronies are very superior to be 'worried' about the Nazis' attitude to women. They are 'worried' about the 'inferior' position of women in Ireland? The countries where women occupy the superior position—their names and some indication of their prosperity would be welcome. Of that Mr O'Faoláin himself gives one hint:

Take one European country, for example—Sweden. Between 1850 and 1930 the number of people engaged in Industry and Mining grew from 8·5% to 37·3%. That is why women in that country go into employment. That is why here they scrub floors or feed hens.

Well, that's clear enough, anyway. In the enlightened countries, the superior position of women is affirmed by sending them to work in the mines. It is reasonable enough, in a way, but could they not find time to scrub floors before going out in the morning? We all know hens must be fed. Does Mr O'Faoláin suggest that this is a peculiarly male office? Does *he* feed hens and scrub floors? And assuming we want to give our women a superior status, as in Sweden, how can we do this if we haven't any mines? The *idea* is good here, but Sean hasn't worked it out. He then says:

It is in small things that one sees woman's inferior position here. How many women do you see at a dog track? In Britain they go out with their husbands and have a quiet and sedate beer in a pleasant pub . . . How many women are elected to the Dáil? I think that there has been once a woman Mayor.

Bless my soul, dog tracks are choked with women clutching two bob bets and getting in people's way! Mr O'Faoláin wants them to booze also, and meddle in politics! Apparently his programme for *my* wife is something like this:

6 a.m. – Rise and go down the mine.

5 p.m. – Dine alone at minehead canteen, meet husband so he
can pay for drinks in pub up to 7 p.m.
7 p.m. – Dogs.
9 p.m. – Cumann.

A fine and a full day if you like, very superior also, no
doubt, but I notice it is destitute of any reference to MY
DINNER! It does not treat either of the gastric ills of little
Deasmumhan.

Frankly I think that, out Santry way, we'll leave things as
they are, and risk the 'worry' of Mr O'Faoláin's friends. I
don't believe the mammy *wants* to be a miner, number one.
Number two, I won't stoop to feeding hens for the full of a
field of Sean O'Faoláins! As for scrubbing floors, I'm going
to be terribly nasty: one doesn't *scrub* parquet!

I haven't come into town from my house in Santry for a long
time; in this uncertain weather I am afraid the horses might
get restive and spill me out of the landau. (I'd try the
waterau if there were more canals here.) Hence it is that I
haven't stood in a Dublin theatre for twenty years. True,
Hammy Benson has made it known that he will with pleasure
give me a box any time I look into the Gaiety, which is very
kind of him. (Didn't say what sort of box, though; a box on
the ears wouldn't quite suit me at my time of life!) But quite
free, quaintly, I have theatre folk out to dinner and I listen
to their talk; that keeps me in touch.

I am terribly interested in the American theatre, particularly in the bright insouciance of its lighter mood. There is
a heart-lifting pertness in the lyrics of the show now running
at the Gaiety Theatre. How delightful the opening one 'Oh
What a Beautiful Morning!' (And very witty the gagging that
wheels our revered film censor into the first line of it—
'There's a bright golden Hayes on the meadow'!) Is there
man so dead as will not surrender to the charm of that second
lyric 'How are things in Glocka Morra?' I suppose we have
here and there a pseudo-intellectual ba*d who is very
superior about this sort of play. Permit me, as one who has
done much to define and maintain taste here, to assert that
Somerset at the Gaiety Theatre is an original and charming
work. Why has the Dublin Corporation hidden from us so

long the bright talent of Alderman Meredith, of whom, until this week, my Excellency had never heard? What insane negligence has prevented somebody from presenting Pauline Goddard, the Rt Hon. Burgess's wife, at my house in Santry? I would have been delighted to throw a *chérie* party. (Could have asked Garrett, too, who has rather discourteously kept away from me since his arrival. Let me here counsel him to listen to no tales.)

I am very pleased to hear that *Somerset* is going over big. But I am not so pleased to think (*frowns thunderously*) that steps had to be taken to see that the show was not sabotaged before the curtain went up. Is this a democracy here? Is the pursuit of happiness guaranteed? Begob I sometimes wonder.

The facts of a very scandalous business were set out in last Sunday's issue of the London *People*. The *People* is a great British newspaper dedicated to the political, athletic, spivic, astrological and erotic indoctrination on Sundays. The editor is by no means stand-offish, and openly calls his readers 'chum' and 'ma'am'. The complicated subject of love is every week the subject of extended exegesis, and many discoveries are recorded. Last Sunday's treatise, for example, opened as follows: 'Out of the consulting room of a famous Harley Street psychologist has come a lesson for modern prac-titioners—"*You Can't Always Card-Index Love!*" ' (Prob-ably true. Suppose you could, though? What then? Can't see many people putting in their time at that game. It's too . . . too academic, I think.)

The *People*'s best thing is a column written by a Mr Hannen Swaffer, a grand old man with long hair and a kindly sad face. Mr Swaffer has spent a lifetime, if not two, in the service of the Plain Man, carefully supervising the delicate political ritual of moving him timidly to the left. (Perhaps *rubric* would be a better word than 'ritual' there?) Mr Swaffer is in fact a sort of 'Socialist' divine, now full of years and author-ity; his word is law, even in Dublin, as the following remark-able extract from his column will show:

It was not until hours after last Monday's first-night of 'Winter-set' in Dublin that I knew why I and three other London critics had been invited to fly to it as guests of the management.

True, Burgess Meredith, now a film star, was repeating the performance which made his Broadway fame in 1935; and equally true, Paulette Goddard, his newish wife, was making her stage debut 'for Art's sake'.

Then, long after midnight, Burgess came into my bedroom and confessed that he and Paulette had been denounced as 'Communists' who had chosen Dublin for propaganda 'because it is a world capital'. Hearing threats of a boycott by the local newspapers 'because of the Church', he had suggested we should be asked so that he and his wife 'get a square deal'.

At one time during rehearsals, he told me, he thought of throwing up the engagement and returning to London; it wasn't worth the trouble . . .

Picture it, lads. It is long after midnight. The grand old saint is in bed, the jewel-like face reposing in the downy nest of his patriarchal hair spread upon the pillow. Possibly he is saying his prayers ('God bless Mr Attlee and God bless Mr Bevin, and please also keep up the circulation of the *People*. And please find a way of card-indexing love'). Where is his wandering boy tonight? There is on the door the knock of tiny knuckles. Enter Master Burgess in his little dimity night-shirt. He was alive in 1935 and is therefore at least twelve years old. 'Ah my boy, come here.' The patriarch runs his fingers through the boy's golden curls. 'And phwat have they been doing to you at all in Dublin, my little treasureen?' The boy's pretty features wrinkle, and he begins to blub. 'Please . . . please, sir——' (By the way, is this killing you? It's not? Well, it's killing *me*, and we'll cut it out.)

Isn't it a scandalous thing that a boy of twelve should be accused of dabbling in satanic political philosophies and that people should be put to the expense of importing Blessed Hannen Swaffer by air, with three unnamed acolytes, to save him from that formidable combination, the Church and the Dublin newspapers? We certainly live in strange times, but there must be some sanity left when the Church and the papers had the sense to back down when it was known that Holy Swaffer had arrived. Suppose hot-heads in both enclaves had their way and saw to it that the Alderman and Pauline did *not* get a square deal? Begob, I suppose Hiroshima would be small stuff compared to the punishment that

would fall on this town. (Might even have supplies of the
People cut off on Sundays!)

And talk about narrowness! Pauline, according to St
Swaffer:

was guilty of one mild indiscretion. She gave to the theatre
management, for distribution, thousands of signed postcards of
herself that were a shade too risqué for Dublin. The manager,
tactfully, left them in his office.

'The Perils of Pauline' would be a good title for a film of
that rather precarious drama. I think the manager did the
right thing. There was a bit of trouble on another occasion
over the Pauline Epistles.

Let's clear this thing up finally. I think I correctly interpret the public mind when, on behalf of the State, I apologise
for any inconvenience or annoyance that may have been
caused by the Church to Alderman Burgess and the Lady
Burgher (That's O.K., I think? 'Burgess' masculine, therefore 'Burgher' feminine?) I'm personally very glad, Alderman, me good sir, that you thought Dublin worth the trouble
and that you didn't—O dread possibility!—'return to
London'! Your modesty (which becomes more startling when
one considers your endowments as an actor) has won golden
opinions. Your show—'Oklahoma', I think?—is a smasher.
The part of Finian fits you like a glove. May I in humility
suggest a super finale for the closing night? Get St Swaffer
and his three pals back and put them into the show dressed in
brocaded night-shirts and presenting your Excellency with a
square deal. (Deal is a bit hard to get nowadays but T. and
C. Martin will fix you up if you mention mine aim.)

It's very hard to get away from Irish Architecture.

I've just bought a book called *Irish Smiles* by Frank
O'Connor optimistically hoping for a laugh, and find it deals
mostly with the doorways of our ancient ecclesiastical
remains, as well as with the architecture of peasants' faces.
Mr O'Connor cycled about the country in shorts accompanied by ladies with French names, also on bicycles and
clad in jodhpurs. It's one way of seeing the country, I suppose, though it seems to have more merit as an all-out plan

for being seen. There's quite a point there, mind you. If you want to see really clearly, you must yourself be invisible, otherwise you are altering the sum of what you want to see by the addition of yourself. When part of what you want to see is Irish country people in the country, then if your inspection is to have any value you must be, if not invisible, as un-obtrusive as possible. 'A respectable middle-aged writer' (Mr O'Connor's description of himself), in shorts on a bicycle laden with cookery equipment, accompanied by French female cyclists in equestrian rig, with himself getting 'bad falls' in rainstorms owing to moisture on his glasses—nobody but small boys or Englishmen can do that and get away with it. Mr O'Connor was, of course, mistaken for an Englishman. He can hardly complain, since his get-up occasionally deluded even himself. Twice, he found himself 'home-sick for the Strand'. How ignoble—and how futile—to forget even momentarily that one is from Cork! Shure Mr O'Connor even *writes* a phrase like 'eight-century illuminations'. And I see nothing wrong with it. (I like Cork people, by the way.) The Strand be blowed!

Mr O'Connor's book is good in parts, and in parts very good. Some of it is interesting, for reasons unknown to Mr O'Connor. Take this bit, for instance:

It was my turn to look for hot water. There wasn't any, but a motherly woman put the kettle on to boil while I sat in the kitchen with her. A few moments later the back door opened and a little man came in. He was small and wiry and spirited, with a slight moustache and blue eyes that danced with mischief . . .

'You ought to be thankful you are out of this war anyhow,' I said, deliberately drawing him out . . .

There is much more in this strain. Mr O'Connor's is a clinical attitude. He tries to suggest that his relationship with these people is that of a scientist examining his specimens. Personally I am by no means so persuaded. I think the speci-mens have analytic powers at least as good as Mr O'Connor's but functioning much more efficiently, since the specimens are at home in their own kitchen, dressed soberly according to their station, quite at ease and with judgment unimpaired by superciliousness. *What was said after Mr O'Connor left?*

That is the snag in all egocentric writing. Its incomplete-
ness is mortifying. Here there is an entire department of
literary deficiency. Having read the book, why cannot the
reader read the Other Book? I don't suppose one can plan
that sort of thing but the rules of chance will have it happen
sooner or later. Literary man enters cottage, examines
country folk, 'tries' them on various topics, then writes shiny
piece for the *Bell*. Country folk turn out to be repentant
National B.A.s who have reverted to pleasant rustic indolence but who 'write a bit'. One of them records visit of
literary tourists, appearance thereof, attempts to steer conversation into certain channels, awkward exit, etc. Peadar
innocently prints both in same issue. Result: laughs for all.
That applies to a lot of ye writing lads, of course.

The absence of this sort of complementary literature, and
the apparent certainty that it will never be written, tend to
make the stuff that is written so personal and partisan that the
reader usually learns much more about the author than he
does about what the author is pointing at. In Limerick Mr
O'Connor discovers a poster showing a young girl fully
dressed but with a rectangular sheet of paper pasted across
the picture. Mr O'Connor's reaction?

' "Civilisation?" I thought, going cold all over. "Did I say
civilisation?" '

I wouldn't put it past you boy! But this sheet of pasted
brown paper looks to me exactly like the sheet hoarding
proprietors use to cancel a poster when the period paid for
has run out to save the trouble and expense of obliterating it
until somebody else buys the space. That, though prosaic and
unlikely to make Cork cyclists go cold all over, is probably the
explanation. It is perfectly certain that no Irish person with
odd—and therefore very strong—ideas would start carefully
editing an objectionable poster advertising cosmetics. The
whole thing would be ripped and slashed to bits or drowned
with tar.

The other explanation is that some bright person, being
fond of jokes at the expense of terribly serious persons, did
the tailoring job Mr O'Connor sees, possibly having heard of
the London joker who rode on the top of the omnibuses,
loudly giving mistaken identifications to public buildings for

the benefit of a friend and then having violent altercations with dissenting fellow passengers.

'Can it possibly be,' Mr O'Connor inquires elsewhere, 'that Irish people think they are subtle?'

Begor, it could happen!

(I'm surprised to see that Mr O'Connor's work on our old monastic foundations is not published by the Mellifont Press.)

This is Part II of my series, the Roasting of Architects. In Part I we saw that most cities have become dangerous and uninhabitable, and that architects wish to be permitted to remedy these conditions, which have been created by architects.

Forty years ago you could walk up and down the length and breadth of Sackville Street without once meeting an architect or suspecting that such existed. In those days an architect was a builder's assistant, he dressed modestly and respectably, he knew his place and went quietly about his business (which he knew). When Joe Holloway was building the Dolphin, you did not find him swarming about the planks and ladders, getting in the way of workmen, tasting the 'mix' like an old cook, and letting himself down before the builder. When he wished to know how the higher constructions were going, he quietly viewed them from the upper windows of adjacent buildings. The Dolphin is still standing (or was up to Saturday night last). There was a bit of old decency about in those days. I have the relics.

Your young architect of today is a very different proposition. He dresses like a jockey off duty, never appears in public without a roll of what looks like 'plans' but which nobody has ever seen unrolled. He wears a coloured woollen tie (this is a *compulsory* rule of his Institute). He has a point, of course. His point? That he is in reality not an architect at all. He designs, yes. But the primary problems of space are aesthetic, you see. In reality he is an artist. He paints, of course, though if you wish to corner him, well, there's no use in denying it. His ultimate problem is his music. He doesn't play, of course —one doesn't do that nowadays. Or listen to music much. What's the point in listening to Prokofieff when one can read him just as well?

I'm perfectly serious about this. It's no laughing matter. This type of lad has got a feminist psychology, hence his preoccupation with pretty coloured bricks, glass blocks, tinted slates, strange foreign timbers, 'plastic' materials that will submit to sweet fancy in shape, colour and surface. His manipulation of these materials is, of course, frilly, 'poetic' and undisciplined. His is the decorative obsession. Ask him to give you a building and he will go to work on his 'façade', hoping that when that is approved it will be possible to squeeze in some sort of a building behind it. Women are the same. A woman doesn't care if she hasn't a stomach provided she looks as if she hasn't.

And now, back to the Institute's *Year-Book!* One thing about Paddy Solemn, there's nothing easier than pulling his honest leg. Nothing would do the *Year-Book* only send away to foreign parts for a 'message' from wealthy non-national practitioners who are regarded as leaders of the craft by people who do not have to see their buildings or live in them. Two of the replies, which are solemnly accepted and printed without comment, complete with romantic portraits of the authors, are spoofs! Your men Corbusier and Frank Lloyd Wright wink to themselves, write out the most ridiculous leg-pulls concoctable, and mail them to the serious young men in the Institute. Corbusier's joke is so exquisite that it would be mutilated by quotation otherwise than in full:

J'ai passé en Eire le 30 février où l'avion de New-York s'est arrêté une demi-heure à Shannon, et je dois dire combien j'ai été enchanté de votre petit aéroport, modeste mais impeccable [Note: the runways are four miles long], *et de l'hospitalité très propre et gentille que nous y avons réçu. J'ajoute que le survol de l'Irlande m'a révélé un pays qui doit être magnifique à parcourir à pied. J'ajoute encore que, ayant lu autrefois les aventures de* Koulouhan, *fils de chien, qui appartient à votre légende héroïque, je ne puis faire autrement que d'être plein de sympathie pour tout pays-là. Je connaissais James Joyce d'ailleurs, dont j'admire l'Ulysse, mais je préfère* Koulouhan, *et toute cette immense légende qui est au fond de votre histoire.*

Yes, that is very, very funny. Tell you a good word for it—it's Greek but it's damn good—*anakolouthon! Non de chien!* Who but the exquisite architects would thankfully accept

Corbusier's 'message' and exhibit it with the dumb pride of devout incomprehension?

Wright's piece, though lacking the subtlety and grace of the other, will form the subject of our next discourse and will in due time here be examined, to be followed by exclusive and quite sensational revelations touching upon the princely hospitality shown by the Institute to the limey confrères, the extent and richness of the same, *and details of who paid the bills*. (Phew! I can't quite believe the information which in meticulous dossier lies before me, but ... then I am old-fashioned!)

Venio nunc—hould hard, this won't last long!—*ad voluptates agricolarum, quibus ego incredibiliter delector; quae nec ulla impediuntur senectute et mihi ad sapientis vitam proxime videntur accedere. Habent enim rationem cum terra, quae nunquam recusat imperium nec unquam sine usura reddit, quad accepit, sed alias minore plerumque maiore cum faenore.*

These are the words of a man whose livelihood was derived otherwise than from agriculture, so there is no reason why I should not discuss the subject myself. (*Voluptates* is excellent!) (So is *nunquam recusat imperium*, particularly *in Hibernia, olim* (1847)!)

Agriculture is by no means a simple craft, but of this much I am certain: James Dillon is never happier than when trying to make it look more complicated than it is. Usually his bête noire is beet rouge but listen to this extract from a newspaper report about wheat:

Mr Dillon said he had grown wheat on his own land during the emergency but once wheat from abroad was available again he would not be seen dead in a field of wheat on his own land because he knew that the whole rotten fraud had been enacted to promote the Rank interests.

Mr Dillon need not look round for praise when he says he grew wheat on his own land. After all, that's the usual system. Growing wheat on other people's land is probably illegal. The rest of his address, evidently intended to confuse everybody, seems to me to be merely a statement of fact. As a matter of interest I checked up, out in Santry where I have sixty-eight acres of Wilhelmina. All wheat crops grow to a height of between two and three feet from ground level. Assume that the average man has a maximum girth of forty inches (or had before the war); that gives us, when he is lying on his face or back, a maximum elevation of about one foot. In the test I carried out in the presence of two of Mr Rank's cameramen and my own farm steward (an expert, by the way) I waded out into the middle of my largest field of wheat, paused and 'died', and fell on my back. I was completely alone there and could see nothing but the blue sky. Subsequently we went back to the house, got the 'sherry' out and had the affidavits completed. Three men of sound mind *swore* that I would not be seen dead in a field of wheat on my own land. I put that forward as conclusive proof. Or does Mr Dillon claim that he is fatter than I am?

To change the subject (*plus ça change*, one fears) I have been reading a most interesting book about four Soviet 'heroes'—*Life on an Icefloe*—who spent a year in 1936-7 at the North Pole, observing weather and ice conditions. These intrepid Russians, led by one Papanin, were flown in by ski-planes, which later flew in their equipment. Some idea of the latter may be gained from the following list:

The cooking done on two primus stoves, the four scientists undertook in turns. All kitchen utensils were made of aluminium and plastic. For kitchen furniture they had a plywood table and overturned tins. Other articles brought to the icefloe were fuel in rubber drums; a medicine chest; stationery; a small library; spades, pick-axes, crowbars, blowlamps, chessmen, cutlery; canoes, two rubber coats, sleeping bags, small sledges built to a special design; and outfits of Polar clothing, including hooded deerskin coats and deerskin thigh boots, silk and wool underwear, shirts of reindeer skin and sealskin trousers.

Well, these men were sent to observe the weather and after some observation they found it was very bad, so they spent most of their time indoors. But don't imagine life was dull. What's wrong with this for an evening?—

On New Year's Eve Papanin turned barber and insisted on cutting off the long tresses and beard Ernst Krenskel had grown. Then the others shaved and washed their heads before sitting down to a supper that lasted two hours and, beginning with caviare, finished with nuts, chocolate, and thirty-five toffees apiece. They drank a toast to Stalin and for a long time afterwards Krenkel remained at the radio receiver taking down cordial messages from all parts of the U.S.S.R.

The usual round of life was not very different from that. They came in one evening after doing a little bit of 'work' outside:

Back in the tent, Ernst turned on the portable gramophone. Whenever times are most difficult he either sits down to play chess with me or puts on a record.

In the mornings the men were industrious but still urbane:

This morning everything proceeded as usual: Eugene carried out meteorological observations, Ernst transmitted the weather report, and I lost four games of chess to Peter.

Diet? Monotonous? Well, a bit, I suppose, but life was full of pleasant surprises:

During the night Eugene was on watch. A short distance from the hut he saw three bears . . . I killed all three bears with several shots. We are all delighted at this successful bag—we can have fresh meat at least!

Caviare, chess, bear-steaks and 'toasts'—the days passed quickly enough and all too soon, planes and ships arrived to take the four brave men back to Russia. 'On their return to Russia,' the record says, 'they were fêted as world-famous conquerors of the North Pole and made Heroes of the Soviet Union. The Government appointed Papanin, unfaltering leader of the expedition, head of the Central Administration of the Northern Sea Route.'

And very nice, too.

I would be glad to receive a postcard from any person who knows or has heard of, a small farmer or agricultural labourer, in Ireland or elsewhere, who would not regard the life of these Russians as the life of Reilly—who would not regard the 'privations' of these Russians as very heaven. I am also open to receive from readers lists of agricultural labourers who eat caviare, spend most of their time indoors playing chess, or who have ever on New Year's Day consumed nuts, chocolate and thirty-five pieces of toffee.

Finally, if any Irish agricultural workers think it is a bit thick that these four Russians should be made Heroes of the Soviet Union on the strength of having had a year's luxury and indolence at the North Pole, let me counsel them to be patient. The entire population of this country may yet be made Heroes of the Soviet Union. (Ever heard of this new thing the flying saucer? You think it's a *curse*? It's an anagram, anyway!)

A number of people have asked to bring to definitive adjudication the terms of a Proclamation on 'Irish Music' issued some days ago by Mr P. J. Little from my rustic recess of Sandyford. That, I regret to say, is a request to which I cannot axe seed, I beg pardon, accede. (Frankly, lads, I am too busy. At long last I have got down to it. I mean that biography of myself. I am now very busy assembling the materials. Would any person who knows me, or who knew me well years ago, or who has original letters received from me, or who can in any way throw light on my past, communicate with me immediately? All documents will be carefully copied and returned.)

But that is not to say that I am not as ready as the next to laugh at jokes. The following is good, for instance:

A country like Ireland should strain every effort to express its own individuality in music. If we are to follow English models, we cannot expect to be anything but derivative and imitative . . . One must admit that the expression of English music is very limited as compared with European music . . . It is not always realised how much British music today owes to Irish influence. Sir Robert Stewart was the teacher of Stanford, and Stanford was the teacher of many of the most distinguished composers of yesterday, like Hamilton Harty, and of today like E. J. Moeran— and these are Irishmen.

Or, removing the discursive style, put it this way: the work of Irish musicians following English models would be derivative and imitative because English music is largely Irish music; further, Irish music, being largely English music, is very limited in expression but every effort should be strained to cultivate it.

Isn't that a remarkable plea, now? And should one be

surprised to find incorporated in it two statements which are completely untrue—one, that Hamilton Harty was a distinguished composer and two, that Moeran is an Irishman? Poor Harty, whom I knew well, was an accomplished conductor who arranged Irish folk tunes into the form of symphony and, though his work was ably done, it is a great pity he ever did it at all. Names I will not name but if Harty had stayed his hand, then there is a good chance that certain 'Irish' . . . what should one call them—gestures?—of more recent date, all profound humiliations to myself, would never have been heard of—or even heard. A number of 'cellists I know desire to be associated with these sentiments in so far as the 'slow movements' are concerned, and as for those final paroxyms ('Napper's Choice, Shoo the Donkey and Flattery's Bog'), woodwind personnel desire me to state that they view all such matters with grave concern. *And* Moeran is, of course, an Englishman who, unlike Bax or Ireland, does not show any considerable interest in Irish tunes.

There are many other things in Mr Little's address which it would be my duty to consider granted I had the time and granted also that I was sure what they meant. 'All the great works,' he says, 'from Homer to Shakespeare, from Bach to Beethoven, Brahms, Tchaikowsky, Verdi and Puccini and so on are in the mainstream of the life of their peoples.'

Unlike others, I did not have the honour of living in Homer's time, which time is not known, and am therefore unable to question Mr Little's assertion that Homer's work was in the mainstream of the life of his peoples—though there is no denying the thalassic element in his poems. Shakespeare I never met: but I have read all his works and have been impressed, as has every man of good parts, by his abiding unEnglishness, by his presentation of a quality that knows no age or country, one destitute of any recognisable intellectual or social cast, a unique man quite dissimilar to Verdi and Puccini, who were Italian entertainers. Shall I compare him to a summer's day? And Beethoven's work—which he began with the motto *Ars est celare Mozartem*—was in the mainstream of the life of his peoples to this extent, that he was born on the Rhine.

Enough perhaps of quip. I have had a lot of trouble with

this sort of thing before; it arises from either wrong notions or no notions about fundamental matters. In relation to the present question, one has to decide what is art, what is musical art, and who are the artists. What is art? Well, art (we will run through this very quickly, lads) is the production of something that did not before exist, by means of cultivated human skill. *Artium aliud eiusmodi genus est,* said Cicero, *ut tantummodo animo rem cernat.* And again: *Zeno censet artis proprium esse, creare et gignere.* That clear? Narrowing these principles to treat of the fine arts, one sees that such a work connotes cultivated skill in several cerebral processes and postulates a product the like of which never existed before. We thus see that the creation of works of musical art calls primarily for enormous intellectual power and here it is necessary to assert that the artistic intellect has no fixed terrestrial root or site. True, the materials upon which the intellect exercises may be local and bear local hues, the artist himself may physically 'live' in Carrickmines, but his artistic function is scarcely of this world at all. And always the materials will be an unimportant factor. It *is* impossible, mind you, to write a real symphony (say) by manipulating the raw materials of Irish folk tunes (which are sterile unintellected (*elements*)) according to the mystical processes of the artistic pancreas, but the result will not be 'Irish' music. Moreover, it is writing good music the hard way. It is like prescribing for an author the characters he must write about.

But the most important query, for our practical purposes, is the third: who are the artists?

Here we leave theory and abstractions. History shows that art flourishes only in aristocratic civilisations—that is, where human society is ordered by a privileged and wealthy ruling caste housed in cities. This principle was seen to operate from the most primitive slave communities of antiquity right down to our Western world of fifty years ago. How does the principle apply to Ireland? My view is that the Irish have a uniquely strong *instinct* for art. They have sought their cities by pouring across the oceans of the earth and have notably in America, sought to make *themselves* the privileged ruling class. But instinct is not enough.

Here in Ireland today, I do not conceive that art can exist much. You have, of course, no cities here—though that would not discourage me completely if I could descry any considerable body of city persons, however cityless. But one gets back eternally to this distaste of the Irish farm lad for farming. If these people could be kept on the land, I think there would be sufficient wealth here to maintain modest city settlements. What have you instead? You have all manner of offices, shops and factories cluttered up with refugee peasants, all dressed up to the nines, not a few of them got up in Treasury pants and all very busy at their 'work'. Not a few of them are busy rationing the dribble of food that is still produced by the handful who stayed behind because they were too lame or old to run. And mind you, if there was even a remote prospect of urbanising these people (in the art sense), I would not mind. But no, they deliberately withhold their allegiance from the city. They are all, if you please, exiles— exiles from Kerry, Tipp, Monaghan and so on. They band themselves into Kerrymen's Associations and the like for the better safety of their County Council morals. And, of course, they go 'home' at Christmas and Easter, when they know their relatives are likely to have shop-purchased food. A country of city-dwelling city-haters, that is what you have. Was ever so monstrous a perversion? Mr Little apparently calls it 'Ireland's own individuality' and asks that every effort should be strained to express it in music. Heaven forbid!

One other small point. Mr Little talks of the necessity for 'inspiring our musicians to steep themselves in the great classics . . .' It is perhaps because I know a few dozen Irish musicians that I find that word 'steep' a wee bit cruel.

I wish to acknowledge with many thanks the messages of sympathy I have received, and in such abundance. It occurs to me, however, that there may be one or two unperceiving persons on this orb who have not noticed that *every single time* I choose to write a little article on poetry—nay, even poetry itself—under the pseudonym 'Austin Clark', I am instantly most cruelly attacked by Mr Sean O'Faoláin, a man who lately did not scruple to assassinate certain young men whose crime was that they spoke the Gaelic tongue. I am then . . . Pre-Raphaelite? I could, of course, make mirthless jokes about Sean O Raphaelain but nothing—absolutely *nothing*, mind!—will induce me to be bitter or resentful. I'll churn the other teak, as usual, and proceed to an appreciation of Mr O'Faoláin as a writer.

Take that fine book he wrote on my ancestor O Neill. He showed me the proofs and asked for my O.K., which was a decent enough gesture by one who, after all, might have published his work *without* consulting me (it has been done, reader, I name no names, but Mr F . . . k O'C . . . nn . . . r will know who I mean.) (Whom? Hardly.) I did not, of course, read either the proofs or the book itself but I would not be surprised to hear that they contain this passage:

Thus, though we do not know what they thought, that night at Whitehall in 1511, when O'Donnell knelt before Henry VIII to be made a knight, for all that Holinshed says is that he was a powerful Irish prince, we do know what they thought twenty years farther on in the century when the famous Sean O'Neill (1528–67)—the uncle of our O'Neill, known as Sean the Proud, and the first man to be called Great O'Neill—visited the spangled court of Elizabeth in 1562 . . .

I know exactly what Mr O'Faoláin means—fifty-one years *isn't* really much more than twenty years, particularly when you're a writer, as, indeed, who isn't, but still (and all) *ordinary* people might misunderstand. I'd change that before the book is published. Just a suggestion, of course. By the way, how terribly . . . what shall I say? . . . unturgid is Mr O'Faoláin's prose! I mean, it practically reads itself, doesn't it?

Champaign is supposed to be very scarce, but go to those proofs and I suspect you will find plenty of it! E.g. p. 17, 'a dew-wet champaign' (fair profit on that I'd say) and same page 'southward the champaign fades'. Then p. 39 'the vast uncontrolled Ulster champaign', and later, back to 'the great champaign of Kildare and Leix stretching away'.

Another entertaining feature of Mr O'Faoláin's presentation of the story is his lavish employment of soldiery of exotic character—at one point he drafts some 'land-vikings', sepoys are called in at pp. 157 and 164, and, regardless of expense, 'janissaries' (from Scotland, needless to say) present themselves at p. 66. It makes the thing very colourful, very natural and very unaffected. Generally speaking, Mr O'Faoláin's way of writing is most elegant and pleasant to read, at times, indeed it is exquisite. Example: 'Tyrone was like an eighteenth-century Daniel O'Connell—both Renaissance figures, calculating, whorled with reservations, a humming conch of arrière-pensées . . .' How good that is! And Mr O'Faoláin's main point—the superior intelligence and arrogance of his central character—is so well brought out! I quote (p. 140): 'He began to cry as he recited the great goodness of the Queen, and how kind she had been to him, and he wanted nothing but to be faithful to her . . . Then more weepy lamentations began.' P. 141: 'But at those words "for ever" Tyrone broke out into a fresh wail of tears.' P. 239: 'We can imagine the sob of rage and misery with which Tyrone heard that piece of news.' P. 270: 'On his knees he received his rebukes and instructions . . . he was weeping openly.' P. 281: 'Then the chuckle breaks into a sob and the broad body falls on the table crying as helplessly as a child.' Mr O'Faoláin goes on in this admirable strain but at p. 273 pauses to remark, very pertinently: 'Moore was struck by Tyrone's strange display of emotion, so unusual in so undemonstrative a man.' Quite.

I was very pleased about Mr Duggan's speech the other day; it was so terribly *right*, one felt. The price of liberty, Lincoln said, is eternal vigilance. Readers should never forget that great truth. Freedom does not disappear overnight: it is slowly nibbled, eroded, gradually diminished. And it is always attacked where it resides—not in the flummery of flags or anthems—but in the breast of the ordinary citizen. That is where freedom lives. And all is not lost in the land if there yet be raised e'en one lone voice crying loud in the interest of that ordinary citizen. For such a voice has almost a divine majesty. Mr Duggan is vice-president of the Incorporated Law Society of Ireland and he made it clear that where the rights of the ordinary citizen are menaced, he does not hesitate to address stern rebuke to the august Legislature itself. Let me with undisguised approval quote from the newspaper report:

> The powers given to the Agricultural Credit Corporation to recover money due, without any Court order, were criticised by Mr W. L. Duggan ... 'From the point of view of the ordinary citizen,' said Mr Duggan, 'this is a deplorable attempt to invest a statutory corporation with very drastic powers to collect debts due to the corporation, powers which the ordinary citizen would not be allowed to enjoy ... It is certainly to be hoped that, for the sake of the preservation of the rights of the ordinary citizen, no further efforts in this direction will be made by the Legislature ...'

Any ordinary citizen reading these words without feeling a desire to cheer must be a pretty dead sod indeed. They are grand words, they go straight to the heart, and in uttering them Mr Duggan vests himself with heroic stature. I notice with sorrow that the wretched reporter, seeking to assail the purity of Mr Duggan's emotion, pretends that Mr Duggan, in his next words, veered slightly from the subject. The report goes on:

> Referring to the question of increasing the remuneration of the profession, Mr Duggan said ...

That, of course, merely shows the reporter's ignorance. Let us get this matter absolutely straight: *the right to pay fees to lawyers is a fundamental and ancient human right, and is at the kernel of what we know as democracy.* Question that right, diminish it—and what is left of liberty is unworthy of the name. So precious is this right to employ and pay lawyers that where it appears to conflict with common sense or facts, it must prevail. This principle is very lucidly expounded in Mr Duggan's words. He does not treat of money *claimed* by the Agricultural Credit Corporation and recovered without any Court order, but of 'money due', and 'debts due' to the Corporation. I can supply an illustration from my own experience. Some years ago I placed £5,000 in the hands of a solicitor, charging him to invest the money in the interest of a 'niece' I had at the time. (Charming girl, by the way.) The solicitor did a very extraordinary thing. *He took up residence in the South of France and refused to answer letters!*

(What harm but I could have sworn he was Irish of the Irish and would never forsake the old land!) Naturally, I reported the facts to the Royal Incorporated Law Society (of Ireland) who, in a gesture of terrible wrath, instantly redressed my little grievance. Without as much as a court order *they struck the blighter off the rolls!* (Means he can't practise in the South of France, I suppose?) And mark this—they did not insult me by offering to refund my £5,000 on the specious ground that they had given the solicitor their *cachet*, authorised him to 'practise' and to hold himself out to the public as a reliable home-loving man. Not at all—for to do that would be to make a determination on a matter involving money 'without any Court order' and thus would be to violate the principle we have seen above: it would interfere with my indefeasible right to litigate. Their attitude, correctly, was this: if I was aggrieved, I had my remedy: *I could place the whole matter in the hands of a solicitor!* (All these things are very simple, mind you, when you examine them.)

I was sorry that Mr Duggan, when chastising the Legislature, did not say anything about its Sinn Fein Bill. *There* was a scandalous business if you like. That document, for all its elaboration of verbiage and arcane obscurity, was a solemn affirmation of the following uncomplicated proposition:

Lawyers are predatory parasites.

We are seriously asked to believe that a fund worth some £25,000 must not be litigated because, perhaps, £20,000 of it would be 'absorbed' in 'costs'. What an absurd and unworthy attitude! Where now is the legislators' much-vaunted lip-service to the principle that payment of fees to lawyers is a transcendent human right? Has the ordinary citizen no longer got the right to spend his life amassing estates, funds and trusts for division among lawyers, a right which has been the jewel and the glory of human freedom immemorially in every civilised society? I will say no more about that, but we live in strange times, the ancient values are questioned in the most unlikely quarters: it is at least heartening to the ordinary citizen to see the silhouette of the Royal Law Society on freedom's embattled bastion.

There is one bright spot, however. The pay of their

honours, our excellent judges, is to be raised. Five thousand
pounds per annum is the figure mentioned, I think—and it is
not half enough. (You just couldn't *buy* the wisdom and statements—so frequently on points unconnected with law—
which descend from the Irish bench.) Still, it has been
customary to make some nominal allowance to these wise
souls and on that subject there is, I fear, very widespread
misunderstanding. No later than last Saturday the Rt Hon.
Graf Nichevo put his feet right into it, with the following
fantastic paragraph:

> I am glad to see that the judicial salaries in Ireland are about to
> be raised; for it is absolutely essential that men who are entrusted
> with the administration of justice shall be free from financial
> embarrassment of any kind . . .

That hardly makes sense from any point of view. (How
about that solicitor who went abroad with my £5,000?) Graf
Nichevo seems to think that judges should be paid to be
honest, and that otherwise they would become corrupt. But
thousands of other people who have power, and endless
opportunities to be dishonest, are not paid on that basis. And
pray what is this 'financial embarrassment' that is feared? I
am well acquainted with many of our justices and of their
origins, social standing, and the way of life before their elevation (I say nothing of education and ability) and I think it is
fair to say that *simplicity* is the word that affords the keynote
to their personalities. In all conscience they were temperate
creatures and if groan from their tables was ever heard, it was
surely from repast of faultless boxty with, if aught hard-by,
then the crystal glass of Adam's ale. I suppose a pound a week
would see them through. Is it suggested that such men, with
three or four thousand p.a. on the bench, are in danger of
financial embarrassment? Must they, simply because they are
judges, discard the habits of a lifetime, diet upon oyster and
black sole, with, perchance, a carafe of antiseptic Chablis
upon the board?
Let's be serious, for heaven's sake. The pay of judges is
very simply calculated. It is long accepted that citizens have
an obligation of public service. A State must have judges and
judges must be recruited from practising lawyers. It is some-

what of an honour for a lawyer to be offered a judgeship, and naturally acceptance of the offer will entail financial loss. The rough rule is to offer a salary of about half the estimated annual earnings of the lawyer to be honoured. (There is a pension right, of course, which evens things up a bit.) A district justice with a salary of £2,000 would thus be a man who would otherwise, by his own talent and efforts, be earning £4,000. That clear? (I told you before that all these things are pretty simple when you get down to them!)

But lads, look out for that ordinary citizen! He's rather essential, you know, and the best in the world!

I see where Father Felim O Briain was again trailing his coat in the Mansion House the other night on 'the Liberal Ethic'. Naturally, Mr Sheehy Skeffington was present. Both gentlemen are dogging a fled horse. When the alleged controversy was in full career in this newspaper, I was minded for a moment or two to perpetrate a necrophilic invasion, i.e., enter the Liszts—and maybe remain there *per dracula draculorum*. With my accustomed insight, however, I perceived that the thing wasn't a controversy at all, and naturally I had no business there. Father O Briain did not argue or express opinions—he merely expounded dogma. In that regard he was well-advised, for he once did express opinions —on the revival of Irish in a Gaelic League publication—and my hand is on my heart when I aver that never have I seen wilder or more baseless nonsense. Mr Sheehy Skeffington is a different type: his matropatronymity announced the fact. He is urbane, mentally fearless, more preoccupied with the underdog than with dogma, probably of slight build, tweedclad; he hates caste so much that he lives in Trinity College. Both he and Father O Briain share equally one startling quality: neither has the slightest chance of being seated at dinner in Santry Great Hall. For why? Do I dislike them, think them tasteless in dress? Not at all. I am afraid of my life of being bored.

Yet that correspondence in these columns was interesting for an odd reason. It amounted to a re-statement of a perfectly ludicrous proposition which has been almost universally accepted not only in Ireland, but throughout the world. It may be expressed in a number of sub-propositions:

1. A person born in Ireland who is a Catholic and who possibly harbours nationalistic sentiments is a low mean stupid dog; he is superstitious and priest-ridden, is forbidden to read any worthwhile books, particularly the Bible; he gratefully lies down under all the most outrageous tyrannies, and even keeps inventing new tyrannies; he is a fool as well as a helot; he is an ignoramus; he is the divil altogether for sex but studies the thing from afar, as he would the sun, with enormous caution; he is incapable of any artistic performance or appreciation; he is, in fact, the laughing-stock of the world.

2. A person born in Ireland who belongs to one of the Protestant denominations and who realises clearly the importance of the British connection—being, he hopes, no whit the less a good Irishman for that—is a highly cultivated person whose wise eye ranges rather the intellectual *massifs* of Europe than the homeland's quaking bog; in person he is suave, elegant, accomplished—but where freedom is menaced, where his workpeople are caught buying or selling indulgences, then behold ferocity most frightrous. He lives in Ireland because he has a mission here (that of preserving life's graces, tending the flame of freedom in the national mind) but sometimes he lives in Paris, like Mr Frank MacDermot. All Irish works of art have come from his breed; he is the declared enemy of profiteering, fascism, pauperistic State practices, vice, drunkenness, slums, illegitimacy, and all manifestations of neo-Gaelic obscurantism. Some of his best friends are Roman Catholics. He abhors censorship of books, cries for books in great profusion but must reserve as a matter for his personal judgment the right to censor children (pre-natally, mechanistically). He has not got and does not need a job.

3. The most outspoken and fearless paper in the whole world is the *Irish Times*. Comment is free, it holds, but facts are sacred. Its columns are open to all. Its team of writers is the highest paid in Europe.[1] Its liberal eye emits a piercing

[1] When I started to write this article I knew it would get funnier as we went along.

ray in that bourne of gloom, despond and dismay that is the Eire of today.

Well, lads—how are we?

People often ask me what is the true meaning of that word ethics? Ethics, really, are simply applied morals. Kissane of Maynooth can argue the toss till the cows come home (beasts dewlapped, ample-uddered, returning) but *that's what the word means.* I think it follows you can't have any ethics, postulate for yourself any ethical standard, unless you have morals. Most dacent Catholics are born with rather more morals than is necessary; the present writer has thrun out more morals in his day than any man-jack since Parnell.

There is another important point. The moral and ethical codes do not cover everything. If I go into the street, stop the first stranger I meet and deal him a blow in the face with my fist I have committed no breach of the moral law, and it would be childish to accuse me of having a deficient notion of ethical conduct. I am simply some sort of an *enfante de siècle,* that's all—the very type for whom the Church has a warm corner, and always had.

If I may express an opinion—heretofore I have been dealing solely in facts—I think a great number of Irish Protestants are narrow-minded—the inevitable result of being self-conscious on the necessity for being broad-minded; they can be very, very boring and when they exude, like steam, their sense of emancipation, their right to free thought, declare to goodness you are sorry you did not bring your raincoat. But I find that most Protestant clergymen are not like that. Perhaps it is because they are mostly poor and scantily supported by their flocks. Incidentally, I forgot to mention another widely believed notion—that he is *gay*, whereas sullen Paddy is afraid of his life to laugh at anything but smutty jokes. All right, but try spending a Sunday in Belfast, preferably when it's raining.

By the way, there is a very interesting character one meets in Ireland—the spoiled priest. How is it one never hears of a spoiled Protestant clergyman? I must think that one out. The fresh air seems to stimulate cogitation. Thinking a thing in is immensely tedious.

You know, of course, what the present Excellency deems himself to be? A spoiled Proust, of course.

Well, *I've been got at*! I'm not to say any more at the moment about who paid for the Institute's hospitality! The architects are up in Nearmes, a small stone pub on your left on the way up from Ballinteer to Kilmashogue. (This pub, by the way, is made of granite, has rectangular doors and windows, level timber floors, rooms (located internally), a staircase and a roof covered all over with—O horror!—*slates*! There is in the entire shoot not a single asbestos bollard, muffed teak transom, cavity-construction 'relaxation-bay', stainless-steel mantelpiece, or 'deck'. I need hardly add that it was designed and built by a journeyman mason. I once asked him why he did not employ an architect.

'I have to live here,' he said simply. 'The other class of thing is all right to be looked at be the crowd in motor cars.'

'I fear your house is not a social statement,' I said.

'Social statements are uninhabitable,' he replied. 'I call this show "Pauperum Taberna", chiefly because there's *rum* in it.')

Well . . . let's back today to our unfinished meal on the 'Royal' Institute's priceless *Year-Book*.

There is in a place called Taliesin a famous architect named Frank Lloyd Wright. The *Year-Book* several times mentions this Taliesin but never tells where it is. Is it in Dublin? Panama? Or is this something one *should* know? Is it a place of devotional importance, like Rome or Mecca, which makes details of location superfluous? Is Frank Lloyd Wright an Irish architect? If so, has he traded on the vulgarity and ignorance of the simplest class in the community (publicans) and mutilated the interior of Irish pubs designed in a former age by competent builders? How is it that he gets away with two Christian names, like Edgar Allen Poe and Oliver St John Gogarty? Does he speak Irish?

Thank God we are not *completely* in the dark, for the *Year-Book* prints a 'Letter from Taliesin' by a person who is evidently not Frank Lloyd Wright, for he calls himself by another name. (We now know there are at least two people in Taliesin.) This 'letter' certainly doesn't look like a letter—

there's no *Dear* at the beginning or *Yours ever* at the end. Everywhere Taliesin is mentioned in it, it is printed in italics: that is very significant, of course, but the significance eludes me. Perhaps it merely means that Taliesin is a foreign word and should be pronounced Talsan. I know not. But anyhow, the letter-writer starts by disabusing the minds of people who imagine that Taliesin is the name of a Hungarian Cabinet Minister resident in Switzerland. 'You ask about *Taliesin*,' he says. 'Well, *Taliesin* is land . . .' Now we're getting somewhere.

Yes, this letter. He proceeds: 'In *Taliesin*—as you know——'

Thanks for that 'as you know'.

'In *Taliesin*—as you know—there are three main groups of buildings, each growing out of its own land.'

Very inter-esting, indeed! It shows how conservative they are, even in Taliesin. In Dublin, for instance, one would *expect* slavish adherence to the old-fashioned idea that a building should be located on its own site. Personally I can never get over my chagrin to find, day after day, the Unitarian Church in Stephen's Green located in Stephen's Green. It is as bad as having the rooms in my house located *in* the house instead of out of doors, in consonance with the minimum demands of hygiene. I think they might have been a little bit more enterprising in this upstage Taliesin. Sorry, *Taliesin*. Note how small the problem was: there were only three main groups of buildings—and they had to go and have each on its own lands! How simple and tourist-worthy it would have been to give *Taliesin* substance, for a slogan like 'In *Taliesin* no building stands on its own lands but elsewhere.' I am assuming, by the way, that 'each one *growing* out of its own lands' is a figure of speech (or should I say *façade de parler*?). But one would not be surprised that in a place like *Taliesin* they had discovered how to make buildings grow from seeds. Pity they haven't, in a way. For one thing, it would save the faces of architects. A stranger wincing at the sight of some building could be told 'Ah, shure it's only nature.' We would then have a new 'industry' called Tecticulture and buy coloured packets of bungalow seeds from Woolworth's. The Department of Local Government Board would explain its failure to provide houses for the working classes by talking about the bad 'harvest'. Heavy rains had a deleterious effect on house-growing and was viewed with grave concern, we would be told. Yes, a person planting the seeds of the Foxrock type of bourgeois impertinence would no doubt often get a shock at the type, colour and shape of what comes up. But then what word do you use to describe the feelings of a 'client' when brought by the architect for his first look at 'the job', even if the architect has taken the customary precaution of making him half-drunk in town before going out?

But we must not let the *Year-Book* cool. Back to *Taliesin*! What goes on there charmingly told in the grand letter I am quoting. Listen and learn:

> But I promise you—there is no waste—every spadeful of earth, every axe-swing, every chisel-blow, each pencil-mark, all accumulate and distil knowledge under the guidance and inspiration of a great mind and a courageous spirit . . .

Fair enough, but note again this craving for mystifying the reader. Why suppress the names of those two men hinted at at the close of the sentence? But let him continue:

> From these labours comes an innate sense of the integrity of material, firstly in their own structure and growth, and then in the knowledge of their harmony and limits of construction guided by our own minds and hands. And it is this sense which is so surely an honest and intensely good basis to all great architecture—in fact to all art,—because it is a natural truth, which is an essential part of our existence just as much as seeing or sleeping.

Are ye still with us, readers? There's more!

> This is the real root of art—the root of natural and sincere life that grows from God—not from the Industrial Revolution! Integral art that demands no introverted frustration, no withdrawal from the honest life of man or society into the pale loneliness of an unrealistic existence.

D'you understand all that now? Art, begob! Integral art demands no extroverted frustration, eh? You see where we are *now*? Architects are artists and saints! I wonder at what price this art and sanctity cubes out on the job? There's a sequel, of course—*Frank Lloyd Wright has white hair!*

And here he sits with the light shining on his white hair, as eager and fresh as a youth designing his first building. Here is a real man whose mind is full of the beauty of life.

Good! But are we quite certain that he is *not* a youth designing his first building? I wouldn't go too much by the white hair—it may be due to suffering. Also, it is rather jumping to conclusions to imagine that Frank Lloyd Wright *must* be 'a real man' simply because he has white hair. I have a thing out in the house in Santry with white hair on it and it's not a man at all! It's a queer little French bandy-legged sofa richly garnished with white hair 'upholstery', the same being replete with ticks and mites. And certain it is that that sofa never designed a building!

If it is suggested Frank Lloyd Wright is a real man because his mind is full of the beauty of life, then it will in sooth go hard with my Excellency, who is unaware of the beauty of life and is therefore not a real man. I've suspected something of this sort for years. Possibly I am none other than Dr Sigmund Taliesin, a Jewish dialectician born in Latvia now exiled in Florence and engaged in writing Volume XII of his monumental twelve-volume novel, *Der Alte Landvutter*. But that assumption raises the greater problem of what I'm doing *here*. Hmmm. Perhaps we had all better rest. Today has been very arduous.

Politics

Certainly Costello was not lacking in courage when, the other day, he introduced in Parliament his Arts Bill: this I take to be a thinly veiled plan to give Paddy Kavanagh a pension for life. I object, of course. Taking the papal Bull by the horns, I assert it is contrary to Catholic teaching. Number two, I was not consulted. Number three, I am unaware of any artistic activity which has survived the enrotment conferred by public subsidy. The Abbey Theatre is a case in paint. (Yes—*paint!*)

It was different in the old days, of course. In them days, if you were a gentleman you were *ipso facto* an artist and usually you lived in the Vatican but up near the ceilings, lying on your back, painting. Costello is the latest to come out with the preposterous doctrine that the poor—who have the important and dedicated function of being just that—are probably artists at heart who cannot do the divil and all because they have no money. The true artist has no interest whatever in money, usually because he has plenty of it—or if he hasn't, his mother has.

Deputy Sheldon's views notwithstanding, I see nothing morally wrong with the Irish farmer paying rates and taxes instead of posing as an indigent national martyr and living out of the industrious townsman. Still, his refusal to pay anybody or do any real work I accept as inevitable, probably to be blamed at the heel of the hunt on Cromwell. The Irish farmer's secondary and more pernicious perversion is what I am prepared to fight. Hitherto, the Irish farmer's peculiarity has been to get all his sons and daughters into the Civil Service in Dublin. This means, of course, that government business is subjected to the technique of incubation and gestation as practised on the farm. Every few months or so the farmer gingerly tip-toes out, hides a few spuds under an odd scraw, retreats back to the fire (one cwt of turf in full blaze) and resumes the task of spitting, smoking and cursing the dog. Dame Nature will do the rest.

Well, I object to that. Files don't germinate or send forth green shoots at springtime. It's a silly and vulgar idea. But if the offspring of farmers who cannot get into the Civil Service are going to be sent to Dublin in the guise of artists, I will ask the Leinster House authorities for a Joint Session.

At the same time I was interested in remarks made in the Dáil on this whole question. Deputy Con Lehane made the extraordinary point that Ireland is not Dublin. The Deputy, notwithstanding the fact that he personally subsists in an irrevocable paradox (i.e. Con Lehane is Pro Lehane) is perfectly right. Dublin is a Danish, not an Irish city, and will be more so for the next month if certain news about butter is correct. And that remark nearly brings us back to the Irish farmer, who has achieved the prodigy of compelling the Administration to import dairy produce.

But Mr de Valera, who rarely speaks on the subject of art, was excellent. The report says:

Another matter not quite coming under the Bill—he did not know whether the Council could deal with it—was to give scholarships. Deputy McCann had mentioned young ladies sent abroad to continue their musical studies. There should be State provision to help outstanding artists get to the top of the tree.

We tried the idea out in Santry Great Park some years ago, working hand in glove with Flood of the Zoo. We got some Irish artists, including members of the Cork School, and locked them in the Park. Then, with Horan doing the man's job as slipper, we let loose a large maul of timber wolves. I report that the artists got to the top of the tree. (The artists called themselves *fauves*, I think.) Afterwards certain of the ladies asked to be sent abroad to continue their musical studies. I gladly paid the fares, but only after the parties had signed solemn legal undertakings never to return to the Emerald Isle.

I do not know what Mr de Valera's qualifications are for pronouncements on art, but I think some of his statements are a wee bit dubious. The report further says:

A good piece of work required time, and if we were to have really good work, we would have to pay for the time devoted to it, to enable the artist to live and maintain his family *while it was being produced*.

May I say with great modesty that the italics are entirely
mine own.

Is that true?

I don't think so. Considerable works of art are produced
very fast. What takes an awful lot of time is usually a bad
piece of work. The report continues:

> Most buildings today were of concrete. They could not com-
> pare in beauty with a work in stone, but the question of cost was
> difficult to get over.

I don't know so much about that either. Concrete is not a
substitute for stone; it is a *sui generis* medium of its own.
What deserves severe censure in relation to its use is the
fashion of pretending a concrete building is a stone building.

Now look at this rash statement attributed to Mr O Deirg:

> The Irish people were not in charge of their own affairs from
> Grattan's Parliament to the Civil War, and Dublin was the capital
> of a mongrel kind of State, neither Irish nor English.

So far as I am aware the Irish people were never in charge
of their own affairs, and indeed the Act of Union, passed in
1800, gave them more say in their affairs than they ever had
under Grattan's Parliament. I have already pointed out the
sinister symbolism of the location of the Bank of England in
the Old House in College Green. The Irish people are the
wards of two London streets, Throgmorton and Thread-
needle respectively. Mr Lehane had a letter in the *Standard*
recently assailing the 'link' with sterling. There is, of course,
no link. The so-called Irish note IS sterling and differs from
the nationalised British note only in two regards, viz., a
personable shawlie is substituted for the frigid Britannia *and*
the Irish note is printed by aliens.

A final word on this vexed question of art.

Art is awfully important, and is also mysterious. It exists
in a *terra incognita* somewhere between the spiritual and the
material. All great artists are, of course, mute. They do not
execute any works of art because they disdain the essential
vulgarity of communication. They know that their undis-
closed, unperformed and purely abstract artistic prodigies
would be incomprehensible to any but another artist of equal

rank (who does, of course, exist). Such persons treat themselves to the immense luxury of shutting up and go through life quietly and passionately despising the herd. I cannot for the life of me see how that situation is going to be changed by Act of Parliament, and see rather less than no point in Mr de Valera's plea for the encasement of concrete dwellings in stone.

The mute artist I have mentioned may appear egocentric and selfish. Perhaps. But for sheer self-indulgence—letting the intelligent general public in on certain 'works' concerned with the tiniest of tiny thinking—where do you have our nature playwrights and novelists?

What we really need in this country is a few mobile firing squads working hand in glove with an underground police organisation concerned with repatriating to farm work all such refugees from our rural slums who live in Georgian purlieus of Dublin in the guise of civil servants or artists. I have three tractors idle on my land at Santry for the last three weeks and can't get men to work them. The chiners are all in town, painting and writing Dostoievsky's stuff in the Cork argot, or making what they call statchehs of each other.

Dillon, I'll go bail, is behind the whole conspiracy.

Yehudi Menuhin will be in Dublin next Saturday. Fair enough—I intend to ask him a certain question which I have already put to local chiners such as Nancy Lord and Terry O'Connor, i.e. how do you get true semi-tones up high on the E string when it is a question of playing semi, not to say semi-demi quavers? No matter how tightly packed beside each other, two fingers will give you more than a semi-tone. How is it done? From the two ladies I received a fairy tale the length of your arm about 'we do it but we don't know how'! How are you! (*Do* they do it, incidentally? Hmmm.) Readers will sympathise with me in this predicament. Apart from being a lapsed atheist, I am a reformed violinist. In nineteen and thirty-nine Glenavy got on the right side of me and managed to induce me to put five hundred sweet pounds of my dough into Great Northern. No violin-playing since—I burnt my fingers! I now live in seclusion in the Scotch House.

However, to get back to Menuhin, Saturday's papers carried a curious report. The great man was in Lille, France, and after his concert, *he delivered a political speech!* The paper says that he 'appealed for a world government and the harmonious settlement of world discords'. He added: 'Everybody wants peace and a just division of the fruits of the earth.'

I see. Fair enough. On the other hand, two can play at that game. A somewhat terrifying vista reveals itself. How do we know that something like the following will not appear in next year's Dáil Reports, possibly on the Estimates for the Department of External Affairs——?

MR DE VALERA: I think this Estimate must be approached with some degree of caution. There is a certain way of doing things. People may differ one from the other as to the method but usually it is possible for reasonable men to come to an understanding as to the end that is aimed at. We have, so to speak, our terms of reference. Those who advocate a certain course are entitled to their views. Equally, those who advocate a certain other course are also entitled to their views but the sum of this conflict—the resultant—brings us all back to the plain fact that what we are trying to do here, in this House, is to give effect to certain doctrines enunciated through the ballot box by the ultimate authority behind all law, namely, the people of Ireland. It is sometimes not easy to be fair. Heat and recrimination do not add to the work of Parliament. I would like to be fair and to say that the Minister, Mr MacBride, has said and done things which so far as we on this side of the House are concerned, are not objectionable. We do not propose to sit here mute, however, when the Minister permits the public playing of the Beethoven violin concerto.

MR C. LEHANE: The Deputy cannot get used to the fact that the inter-party Government can sit down at a table and do their work.

MR S. MACENTEE: Deputy Lehane may well talk—he swallowed the César Franck violin sonata, canon and all.

MR C. LEHANE: Certainly that remark comes well from the Deputy, a notorious Bartok merchant.

MR D. MORRISSEY: It is a brazen lie that there will be an orchestra in Store Street.

MR LEMASS: Is it in order, a China Chomhairle, for a member to call another 'a notorious Bartok merchant'?

CEANN COMHAIRLE: I did not hear the expression. Deputies must control their tempers. A deputy's speech has been interrupted. He must be allowed to continue.

MR S. MACENTEE: I have no interest whatever in Bartok, or in any other atonal practitioner. I brand the Deputy's insinuation as a lie.

MRS REDMOND: Can you say the same about Prokofiev?

MR MACENTEE: I can, and you can have my share of Hindemith as well.

MR DE VALERA: There are certain values. A man starving to death on a desert island will not despise the coconut. Conversely, a rat will not eat caviare if he has just devoured a dead horse. There is such a thing as a decent and real approach to all problems. Not everybody will have the same approach to a problem. If one does not agree with a particular person's approach, one at least has the right to expound not only the better approach but the objections to the other approach. The facts can be weighed. Certain things can be plainly seen, others perhaps not so plainly. Weighing facts is an elementary public duty. A dishonest approach to facts could only lead to the undermining of the fundamental principles upon which the State as we know it is based. Duty is duty, however unpleasant. I have a document here——

THE TAOISEACH (Mr Costello): The Deputy is no doubt aware that he may not quote a document unless he lays it on the table of the House?

MR DE VALERA: There are certain rules and regulations. There is the question of order and formula.

MR MACBRIDE: Let him read it, whatever it is.

MR DE VALERA: I have here an affidavit which I will lay before the House in due course. It states that at a meeting in Skerries Golf Club in 1935, the Minister put his name to a document asserting that consecutive fifths were admissible in serious music.

MEMBERS: Withdraw!

MR DE VALERA: There are various avenues by which the

truth may be approached and while individuals may choose this way or that, if they reach the truth in the end the path of approach is not material. This affidavit is signed by Frank Gallagher and I have no reason to doubt that what it says is true.

MR MACBRIDE: The Deputy need not distress himself. I still see no objection to consecutive fifths.

MR MACENTEE: I suppose the Deputy sees no objection to that Chopin Polonaise in A?

MR MACBRIDE: I must ask for the withdrawal of that remark. I am entitled to be protected by the Chair.

CEANN COMHAIRIE: I did not hear the remark. There are too many interruptions.

MR O. FLANAGAN (producing oboe): Is the Minister aware that these articles are being openly imported by certain non-national entrepreneurs and will he take steps to have this traffic stopped?

MR DE VALERA: I intend to deal with the oboe scandal in due course. I mentioned the threat to those of us who understand and cherish the sanctity of the family as a social unit, the home as that unit's focus, of this projected performance in public of the Beethoven violin concerto.

MR C. LEHANE: You had sixteen years to ban it. Why didn't you? What about the Haydn quartettes?

MR DE VALERA: There is a certain well-defined method of approach, a means of ascertaining definite facts. I made my attitude to the Haydn quartettes perfectly clear twenty-five years ago. At that time we were concerned to find, in the first place, a means of securing that our people, of whatever walk of life, and without regard to their political allegiances, should have the opportunity, one with the other, of attaining in some measure to the fundamental ideal of——

CEANN COMHAIRLE: Perhaps the Deputy——

MR DE VALERA: I report progress.

It is with regret that I say it but I cannot at this stage reply to the many telegrams and messages which have reached my lodgings on the question of my placing in due course my person at the disposal of the Irish nation in connection with the office of president. A few small technicalities would first have to be considered: I am not, for example, an Irish citizen, though this could readily be remedied by rushing a one-clause bill through Parliament. Moreover, I am extremely busy.

There are, however, one or two observations I should like to make on the relevant constitutional provisions. I regret to announce that the Constitution, your ultimate and fundamental statement of your Irish identity and destiny, is an unconscionably careless document. Some of the English is bad and most of the Irish is disgracefully bad. More, the two languages frequently express dissimilar and mutually repugnant meanings in stating what purports to be the same Article. An analysis of the document page by page will shortly appear in these columns: in the meantime, consider Article 4 (1), which deals with the minimum age limit of candidates for the presidency. People think that one must be at least thirty-five years old, a figure apparently arrived at by an arbitrary bisection of the Biblical three score and ten. Here is the Article in English:

Every citizen who has reached his thirty-fifth year of age is eligible for election to the office of President.

Consider the utter carelessness of that term 'reached'. First, it can be argued that the absence of the complementary term 'or passes' restricts candidature in the case of any individual to one year. Secondly, the word 'reached' establishes clearly that one need not be thirty-five but merely thirty-four! When one has reached one's thirty-fourth birthday, one has then reached one's thirty-fifth year. Was this then what the authors of the Constitution intended? Let us turn (*puts on second pair of glasses over first*) let us turn for enlightenment to the Irish version. Here is the same Article in Irish:

Gach saoránach ag a bhfuil cúig bliadhna tríochad slán, is iontoghtha chun oifig an Uachtaráin é.

I will not trouble you with a disquisition on the colossal inelegance of the phraseology: I direct attention merely to the literal meaning of these Irish words. Here is the exact English:

Every citizen who has completed thirty-five years, he is electable to the office of President.

Thus, you see, you must have completed your thirty-fifth year—reached your thirty-fifth birthday—to be eligible according to the Irish version. According to the English form of the Article first cited, you are game ball at thirty-four! The Irish version prevails. The English version of the Article, which is the only one many people can read, is false and repugnant to the Constitution!

Let me conclude on another point. Why this unique age limit introduced at all? The electors' age limit is twenty-one. Make no mistake about this—*it is a dangerous negation of democracy to have masses of the people voting in respect of an office from which they are themselves disqualified*. This constitutional disability applies to over forty per cent of the total population—some 1,225,000 souls. Probably most of these people will not trouble to vote at all at a Presidential election; they will resent the implication that they are all unimportant juveniles. A man or woman of worth and distinction must be worthy and distinguished long before thirty. The present mania for prolonging adolescence into the forties—one sees signs of it on all sides—must be curbed. If a man can be Prime Minister of England before he is thirty—remember Pitt?—the same man should have at least the theoretical option of being President of Ireland instead. Or should I say 'in addition'?

My political opinions are wall-known. Wall-known is no misprint, mind you—they have been manys the time inscribed on walls in tar and whitewash; and ask me not why tar is not known as blackwash, or why Jack Nugent so resolutely turns his face against that grand delicacy, noir-mange. I esteem and commend all Irish governments, parties, all arcane lodges, dails, oppositions, sinathors—even sacred societies such as the one located at Ely Place in Dublin's only knight-club. And why? Because they are all composed of staunch Irishmen dedicated to agrarian reform (i.e. getting themselves and their friends off the land as quickly as possible), an activity which they rightly call 'politics', a term that means the management of cities.

Should the Nuremberg juridical canon be confined to the aftermath of international and inter-hemispheric upheavals?

Or would it be an idea to have an Irish general election followed by a similar august ritual with the out-going Cabinet in the dock on trial for their lives as criminals? Can you picture the present Cabinet seated in a long dock wearing headphones receiving justice from that revered and supernatural figure, an English judge—one possibly from Belfast? Hmmm? No, the idea is not without its attractions but we must be careful about the *Nürnberganschauung*. Warnings I have already issued on this subject, but owing to the sinful vanity of men they fell on deaf fears. If you defile the waters of true justice and law, you will find to your horror that they have common source and circulation and that they will in time poison yourself. The court ceremonies in Belgrade, centring around Archbishop Stepinac are the first direct fruit of Nuremberg to be widely reported and it has, according to a commentator, 'shocked the whole world'. To be disliked is now a capital office in many countries, and it is even a capital offence to admire another person who is disliked. It is chiefly for his propinquity to Hitler that they will hang Goering. In a book published in 1934 by Elkin Mathews and Marrot Ltd., London, Goering permitted himself to speak of Hitler in the following deliberate terms:

Wherein lies the secret of his enormous influence which he has on his followers? Does it lie in his goodness as a man, in his strength of character or in his unique modesty? Does it lie in his political genius, his gift of seeing what direction things are going to take . . .

[Hmmmm]

. . . in his great bravery, or in his unbending loyalty to his followers? I think that, whatever quality one may have in mind, one must, nevertheless, come to the conclusion that it is not the sum of all these virtues; it is something mystical, inexpressible, almost incomprehensible . . .

In the most generous way the Leader has always forgiven the mistakes of his subordinates. How often has he smilingly passed over mistakes and when pressed, nevertheless, to dismiss whoever was responsible, has often answered, 'Every man has his weak points and everyone makes mistakes' . . .

His unique personal charm holds everyone in its spell. He allows his collaborators the greatest freedom in their own spheres of work and duty. There they are completely independent, and if at any time he really has to intervene if he wants something to be done differently, then he does it in such a way that the person concerned never feels offended . . .

That could just as truly be written about myself or Dev. Is respect for greatness a crime?

It is important to remember that whereas justice (*jus*) has grandeur not devolving from the simian skull of man, law (*lex*) is a human institution and therefore in many respects ridiculous and perverse. A district justice, himself a noted drunkard, sentencing a workman who got drunk on Saturday night could be an example. But all that is inseparable from the ineluctable imperfection of humanity, and the various bodies of statute and other terrestrial law are the best vehicles of justice which can be devised. Where are you if you are concerned to corrupt your body of law, devise retroactive penal codes, conduct trials in foreign languages, refuse to compel the attendance of essential witnesses? You are in the dock.

No, lads. We have as yet seen only the first act of the Meistersingers of Nuremberg, revered home town of Dr Faustus.

I was much taken (and that reminds me of my numerous arrests, with equal number of brilliant escapes, during the Tan war) with a statement made recently at Westminster by Mr Dillon. The newspapers reported the speech as follows:

If the Government would only take off the taxes and burdens Fianna Fáil had placed on agriculture, then agriculture would be able to carry the rest of the country on its back.

A comment occurs to the past writer, pardon, the present writer: could not the Government be induced to . . . make peace with Messrs Fianna Fáil? Shake hands and be fiends? I am not too happy about this Irish idea that tillage is essentially an . . . alien, non-agricultural, probably urban pursuit. I am not too clear as to what these taxes and burdens are and—if burdens be deplorable—why they should be removed so that another and probably more grievous burden should be imposed, viz., 'the rest of the country' planted square on the back. And that term 'the rest'? Is it suggested that agriculture is part of the country, the ... the ... spiritual side of Ireland, say? But I have interrupted the Deputy: he continued:

This country has no natural resources whatever except land and water, and a great deal of the water is in the wrong places ...

Halt! I agree and I list the places in the following schedule for the attention of discerning readers. Places as follows:

(a) Knees; (b) Brains; (c) malt 'whiskey'; (d) all places being places other than places wherein located are hydro-electric machinery installed by the Electricity Supply Board; (e) turf; (f) milk; (g) native timber, fully 'seasoned'; (h) basement of my residence, etc.

It follows, of course—and in this too I agree with Mr Dillon—it follows that a lot of the land must be in the wrong places: Ireland itself, for instance, so placed that the majority of the inhabitants have to spend large sums on ocean-going liners. Agree I cannot, however, that land and water are the only resources of Ireland. What about genius, for example? Is not the Deputy himself not one of the first water? (Myself? Well, I am in rather a different category. You see, it's rather difficult, but I happen to be a genius of the first ... land.)

In sharp contrast to Mr Dillon's pronouncement, here is a statement attributed to another deputy at the same session and which I crave leave to coat:

At present between thirty and forty nations were sitting down at San Francisco trying to decide what the economic life of the world is to be, and this country had as little say with regard to what was happening there, or what was going to emerge from there, as the man in the moon ...

That is pretty well perfect and I do not think I can add anything to it in any way, except to protest against the disrespectful references to myself at the end. Granted I am usually in the moon, *but* that is not to say that any decisions affecting the economic life of the world (of all places) could possibly be taken without my full privity and consent in writing. I have been kept informed throughout and if need be, I will not hesitate to visit the Conference in person one of these days. And I promise that if I do go, these nations will not be long sitting down. They will be sitting up. (Voice trails off as speaker is obscured by heavy cloud.)

Right off, I make the claim that I think the best English in the world is spoken in this House.
    —Mr O'Donnell, T.D., in the Dáil.

Yes indeed. Also, the statement absolute has a very arresting kind of charm. If, for example, I say (as I am sick and tired of saying) that I am the most beautiful man in the world, the world is delighted to encounter a statement so complete, so destitute of qualification, so recognisably perfect and true. If I affirm that Cora Sumper looked to me, the last time I laid Eisenhower, to be an ill-looking but dictatorial frump, I perceive on all sides gestures of assent. Very well. We now come to this point—is it proper for persons other than myself to make such statements? Here we are on dangerous ground and few would be so rash as to venture an affirmative to such a query. Is any person, not being myself, fitted by vast age, by compendious possession of the terrestrial knowledges, by infinities of wisdom, thus to speak of perfection? Quite not, I fear—there is ever the danger that the common man will either mistake the fact, or comprehending it, fail to propound it with the requisite precision. Mr O'Donnell is, of course, an admirable man but if you reread his *alloquium,* you will find that, conscientiously avoiding to claim anything, he makes the claim that he thinks something: I am afraid that that is bad English and I am not surprised that, beginning with a covert side-kick at my Eminence (i.e. *suppressio veri*—'I do not like to mention names, but I think that without exception, from the Taoiseach down, the very best English in the world is spoken here'), he goes on 'to make a cruel' and bitter attack upon me: 'I heard an Englishman comment on a very famous broadcaster. He has made a wonderful impression in England, and he is a glorious talker. One can understand every syllable that man utters, and it is a pleasure to listen to him ... I say he is the best broadcaster in the world.' Why, you ask me, should I take offence at being praised? That is quite the point—the reference is purportedly to one Michael

O'Hehir: of whom, alas, I have never Hehired. Is it not the limit? (Ah, the old bitterness is still there, I fear.)

These deplorable remarks arose out of a discussion in the Irish Congress of the Radio 2RN, a concern which is—let it be said at once—a credit to your postmen. Other deputies, sensing the danger of offending me, wisely confined their remarks to opinions and statements of taste. Here, for example, is the opinion of Mr Hughes:

> We do not want any highbrow stuff here. We want to cater for our own people who have simple tastes and possibly right tastes because they are simple . . .

There you have what is really rather an aspiration than a fact; I doubt very much whether your own people in fact *have* simple tastes and I am unsure also as to the unsimplicity of bad tastes: even a comparatively simple taste which is fairly universal among your own people, viz., the taste for Irish malt served in green glasses about a quarter of an inch thick, with dosage repeated nine times within the hour for five or six hours—that simple taste leads to other matters quite complicated, e.g. the interment of live farmers of advanced years, removal of limbs from live bullocks, drunkenness, etc. I note in passing (sniggers, duly passes) I note in passing that the *patres conscripti* tend to a uniformly global view. What is good is the best in the world. One Mr B. Corish, though not explicitly treating of 'highbrow stuff', declares:

> I consider that Radio Eireann is one of the few broadcasting stations in the world where there is a real effort made to disseminate culture not alone to Europe but to the whole world.

Brave words, but perhaps to be considered in context with Mr Oliver Flanagan's courageous declaration? This:

> Personally, I very seldom find time to sit down and enjoy the Radio Eireann entertainment, but when I do, the only programmes that interest me are the sponsored programmes and the racing commentary.

And now hear Mr Cafferky:

> The programmes as a whole are pretty good. I am not in a position either to praise or to condemn them . . .

I do not attempt to interpret that mysterious comment but hasten to present another passage from his speech which contains, at the end, about as bold a claim for your radio as has ever been yet made:

Most people like to read the newspaper while they are at their breakfast. That gives them time to digest the meal properly. The same effect, I think, would be produced if there was an early news bulletin. It would be almost as pleasant as listening to the birds singing in the early morning. Some people may get up in the morning with very sore heads after the night before. If they were able to turn on the wireless before leaving the house, it might help to change their whole outlook for the day . . .

This passage has at least two possible meanings. One, too fantastic to be acceptable to me, that an Irish gentleman, perceiving himself of a morning to be in the jigs from imbibement of sundry potstill malts, can readily expel the toxicants which pollute his bloodstream by listening to an inexquisite early morning news bulletin by Radio Daring, complete with bomb-shell that Dept. of G.P.O. are about to erect a telephone kiosk at Dublin Cattle Markets—the latter an item once actually broadcast *urbi et orbi*: the other—and this does make some sense, I admit—that it is possible for the aforementioned gentleman to feel at least a little better by turning on the radio full blast as his last act before quitting house so that sullen wife will suffer severely, at least for so long as it takes her to get to the set.

I, who have for so many centuries presided personally over the destinies of the very reverend the people of Ireland, cannot and will not pretend to be unmoved by the great news which from the grand mother country of Britain has just come to hand, bringing words of cheer and encouragement and abundant promise of good things in the daze to come to all good men who in this green clime dwell. There has been, it appears, there has been formed and established within the ranks of the Mother of Imperial Par (laments!), Co. Westminster, a little enclave, a few Jems set in that silver See, a small but select coterie, whose O'Vowed object it is, once and for all from the chains of the rt hon. the O'Pressor to emancip8 the gallant and indomitable company of the Royal Gaels, Southern Irish Divn. There has been set on Foote (Co. Dingle) a distinguished club, gathering within the esoteric circle of its élite all that is brightest and best in the British political harena, and holding always in most genuine O'Steam those pitiful nomadic hordes of displaced personnel which, Vorlach of Faub-Badenheim, we do not deem it unfitting to denominate as the Irish, traditional and time-honoured fusiliers! (Some of them are still doing it—the others are marking it.) Let me at, or on, this stage quote the report from which I have had the honour to deduce these glad tidings, be they high-tidings or ebb-tidings:

'We realise that we may have a little difficulty in the Northern Ireland side, but we are confident that the common man in Ulster will see something beyond religious prejudice and that he and the man of Eire will realise their common interest,' so said Dr H. B. Morgan, Chairman of the Friends of Ireland group of M.P.s last night . . .

The report (for report I deem it to be!) goes on to say that the majority of the group are not Irish (naturally—for how could Irish people be Friends of Ireland?) and that their 'idea is to cement' their 'friendship with people on both sides of the border and to bring them together in Labour Party policy . . .' I am sorry, but that will never do. You will not make a job of it with cement, *annyway*, but to contemplate using, for the purpose of that particular feat of masonry, an aggregate uniquely composed of people—that . . . that, I hold to be barbarous, illegal and totally unwarranted by our previous experience of the nature of friendship. *Virtus, virtus, inquam, et conciliat amicitias et conservat. In ea est enim convenientia rerum, in ea stabilitas, in ea constantia, quae cum se extulit et Ostende!—it lumen suum! Amicitia autem nihil aliud est nisi summa consensio omnium rerum.* But not cement.

Let me add that the whole question of being a Friend of Ireland is most offensive! That is to say that men—unknown to you—should constitute themselves your friends, present you with their unasked-for love, and send unique notice to you through the medium of the newspapers! Are you then an object of pity? Devoid of scaled-down assets? Devoid of exquisite airports, bountifully infested with Skymasters? A Labour Party of your very own? Your own democracy even? Devoid of the common man in Ulster? Dev-oid? Ah no, that will not do at all, I fear—I cannot permit it in any circumstances. (And what is all this about religious prejudice and the common man in ulsters? Why not wear just an ordinary overcoat like the one I have, long black garment belted *twice* (at waist and knees), fly front, velvet choler and astrakhan cuffs? Begob you won't contract much religious prejudice in *that*!)

That Mr de Valera should be talking about film stars came as a great shock to a man of my generation. (A man of my generation? I mean, of course, myself, but I am too proud to say so. What, by the way *is* my generation? Fifty cigarettes for the first reasonable guess.) What are film stars *étoile*? Why not film comets, film planets? (You, Schrödinger, distinguish between 'comet' and 'planet'; discuss briefly the basis of my claim that I am the man in the moon (ten marks).)

Here is an important announcement. *I* wasn't brought over to London by Mr J. A. Rank, given sweets, had my little wheaten head patted by blonde actresses, or 'stood' four vanilla ices in the Dorchester Hotel. It follows, therefore that it is quite possible that I will have something unpleasant to say about the purchase by Rank of important Dublin cinemas so that British films with cardboard sets containing solemn comics like Mr Noel Coward will be shown to Dublin audiences all the year round. Would Professor Busteed kindly step forward? Thank you. Discuss briefly the effect of this transaction in relation to the expatriation of Irish assets (fifteen marks).

Where is Mr de Valera gone? *Come back here!* Sit down! That's the man.

Now . . . where were we? Ah yes, this vexed question of Miss Maureen O'Hara's allegiance. First, let me hint that it is terribly easy for people to put their foot in it, to say the wrong thing. You never know who is related to me. For instance, Miss O'Hara. Miss O'Hara is my uncle! (Oh yes—it *can* be done, I'll tell you how some other day.) Now Mr de

Valera has praised Miss O'Hara (and rightly—she is an excellent girl) but I don't know why. This is what happened:
Miss O'Hara went before an American judge and made certain proposals. The judge thereupon asked her to forswear her allegiance to Britain. Miss O'Hara smiled patiently and spoke more or less as follows:
'But, judge, you don't understand. I'm Irish, you see. It's *Irish* I don't want to be any more, it's allegiance to *Ireland* I want to forswear.'
Is that . . . *nice?* I don't know but I can't quite see that it is any business of mine or Mr de Valera's. (Incidentally, I am a cousin of Mr de Valera's, four times removed; I was put back, of course, but it was a laborious business.) But I am bound to say——
Oh the bould Frank! No, no—come in, it's all right, we're not at anything private. How's all at Sutton? Good. Here, sit over here beside me. That's the man. As I was just remarking here before you came in—isn't our friend looking very well?
But I am bound to say that the proposition that it is possible for an Irish person to be deracinated, by a judge or anybody else, is too fantastic to be even funny. Equally absurd is the notion that anybody can 'become' an American. It suggests, for one thing, that it is possible to acquire the predominant American attribute, i.e. unsurpassed and unsurpassable cheek. The other day, Mr J. Staunton Robbins, described as Vice-President of American Overseas Airlines, was quoted as saying (at the inevitable Rineanna) in connection with tourist traffic:
'I would suggest that your Government get in touch with the I.T.A.'
Would Miss O'Hara kindly suggest on my behalf to the President of the United States that he should get in touch with the Governor of North Carolina about something or other?
(By the way, who will translate *Wieviel Geld hat Göring?* (ten marks)?)

I report that the Lord Mayor, the honourable Aldermen and Burgesses of the Dublin Corporation, subsisting under English Royal charter, are also under a serious delusion. They think they are not already funny enough without getting themselves rigged out in night-shirts (herebefore known as 'robes'), presumably trimmed with vermink. The morning citizen at his humble breakfast of imported foodstuffs, almost asphyxiated by the fumes from his unemptied dustbin, learns from his paper that the night-shirts will cost only £3,000 for a 'set'.

A rather loose estimate, I would say. If it costs £3,000 to enshirt feudally the present ruffians, it should be remembered that our undaunted democratic way of life in nowise excludes the due election of fresh councillors, nor is it lawful to prohibit the election of either giants or dwarfs. Therefore, unless the Corporation is bent on extracting from the ratepayers an extra-sour laugh in respect of new councillors appearing at public functions in grotesquely ill-fitting night-shirts designed for predecessors of dissimilar anatomy, it will be necessary to have several thousand of the ritual shirts made in infinitesimally graduated fittings according to the system adopted by multiple tailors, armies, navies etc. The capital cost of that I estimate at one million pounds today, and I carefully refrain from guessing what tomorrow's price may be. The alternative is to have a set of entirely new shirts made per new Corporation. Indeed, apart from the question of fit (or, indeed, fits), no decent Corporator, appreciative of the lofty standards of his office, would condescend to wear cast-offs.

Why the demand for ceremonial night-shirts?

One explanation may be that the councillors wish to look like Santa Clause, the bringer of peace and love, of gifts.

There is another possible explanation. By asking for this motley, the councillor is in effect saying:

Look, I am not in this job for anything I can get out of it, I am here from instincts of public duty, and to help the suffering poor. I haven't had time to mind my own business, which is now in the hands of the banks. I haven't eaten for two days, not even in the Mansion House. Do you see the suit I am standing in? I dare not be seen in this in public. I only want the robes to hide it.

Still, the principle is dangerous.

If persons voluntarily present themselves for tasks of

public administration, are thereto elected and find that it is impossible to do any business without being attired in fancy dress, *a fortiori* members of the Oireachtas must experience a far more galling frustration. Is it possible that this is really what is wrong with the Dáil? The fellows simply haven't dressed for din?

I don't know. I didn't notice any great change when they put a sort of B.A. gown on poor Frank Fahy, the recently retired Native Speaker.

The desire for robes is really an atavistic phenomenon. Just as in the old days the arts of physic and magic were allied, kings and princes and other public men unified the calling of ruler and clown. Even in the cruder modern societies, the witch-doctor is simultaneously priest, healer, magician and ceremonial clown. The Cork Hill philosophers merely want to become our resident witch-doctors.

(I see that Dr Dinneen, in his Irish–English dictionary, gets in his customary bilingual dig by saying that the Irish for 'gown' is *brat*.)

I suppose those fellows will have their way, and that the rest of us will find the cash. After all, they are the City Fathers. We, I suppose, are the city sons and daughters, and are not yet old enough to know upon what our money should be spent. (Robes, by Gob?)

Indeed, perhaps I should say we are the city wards. And they the healers.

(I did not say *heelers*, mind!)

The meeting of Dáil Eireann today to select a government prompts me to ponder the nature of mace and men, to wonder wherein lies the might of nations.

Today, America leads the world. She has been careful not to disclose where, but her leadership is not to be disputed. The other two great powers are the Soviet Union and Ireland. Why are the three so strong? Why are they noble?

I think the answer is this: *they are not nations* in the homogeneous ethnic sense but racial agglomerates sharing only territory and police forces. An American may be any-thing—a Turk, a heathen Chinee, or a Mayor from Bahoola, Mayo; there is not even a standard skin colour. In the

U.S.S.R. there are ninety-seven acknowledged languages and probably two hundred nations. In Ireland there are thirty-three nations, at least.

Wot makes these organisations tick? (I said tick, not thick.) Where is the real seat of authority?

There is, I think, in the three countries one *dominant* nation—the grown-up nation. And what makes a nation, or indeed a man, adult? I can answer that question with some assurance. It is the quality of utter DISILLUSION.

Take this Ireland. You have various nations—the Orange nation, the Cork nation, the Wexford republic and so forth. They are all immature, and for convenience collectively known as Irishmen. Set in the midst of them, as costly carbuncle in golden frame, is the dominant (and therefore the disillusioned) nation: naturally I mean the Dublin Man.

He is immured in the historic Pale: to him, Ireland is composed of hostile tribes, various rough fellows in the interior, sects, ritual murderers, mystics, provincial university students, poets, Roman Catholics—and every man-jack an idealist. (The Dublin Man rarely permits himself a laugh but the word 'idealist' will always get one.)

Perhaps I might expound this situation by dialogue, like Plato. Let us assume a conversation between an Irish Man and a Dublin Man. The Irish Man is reasonably clean, newly shaved, neatly dressed and good-humoured; before him is a bottle of stout. The Dublin Man has long since discarded all such affected manifestations; he sees nothing to smile at, but rather does he sit in a soiled raincoat grimly contemplating a large beaker containing an amber liquid, possibly cider. The Irish Man opens up with a pleasant inquiry.

IRISH MAN: Well, what is your best guess for Wednesday?

DUBLIN MAN: I don't think you need look further than Martin Molony. He has two mounts. I was talking to a fellow off the B. and I. He is one of the head waiters on the boats and often gets his card marked by the nobs going across.

I.M.: I'm sorry. I meant the elections.

D.M.: The whaaaaa?

I.M.: You know, the elections. The Government.

D.M. (*pallor coming all over face, the eyes free-wheeling*): The ... the Gov ... ment? THAT crowd?

I.M. (*bashfully*): Yes. I was wondering which of the parties is going to get in this time.

D.M. (*mirthless, ghastly smile*): You're oney coddin' me. You're a bit of a card in your own way.

I.M.: I'm serious.

D.M. (*face now blanched*): WHO'S GOING TO GET IN? I wouldn't mind if it was a question of getting into the sea off the Aran Islands where it's four miles deep. *What?*

I.M.: Well, do you think Fine Gael will form a government?

D.M. (*expression of absolute incredulity*): Do you mean the Cosgrove crowd?

(NOTE: The Dublin Man will in no circumstances call Cosgrave Cosgrave. He is ever Cosgrove.)

D.M.: THAT crowd? My dear man, I seen that crowd. I knuwn that crowd very well. I seen them and I seen their fathers. I will tell you one thing about that crowd. That crowd is no —— good.

I.M.: Well, I mean . . .

D.M.: Nor never was any good. That crowd was all Free State Army privates in the old days. For about forty-eight hours. After that the whole crowd was all generals. A crowd from down the country all up in the mess in Portobello drinking Beamish with nothing but braid and decorations all over them and not one Dublin man in the whole bunch, the greatest crowd of impostors and hooks that was ever got together in one bunch, don't be talking to me.

I.M.: But, after all . . .

D.M.: After all WHAT? Wasn't there an inspection once? This colonel walks into the officers' mess above. You lads, says he, are supposed to be officers and gentlemen and you shouldn't be drinking porter with your dinner. And what *should* we drink, sir, says one of the ignoramuses. Well, says the colonel, you should drink a liqueur. The next time the colonel comes round, he finds your men have taken him at his word. A pint tumbler before every man, full to the brim with craym de mont.

I.M.: Really?

D.M.: I needn't tell you, of course, that all that crowd has pensions now.

I.M.: Perhaps you think Fianna Fáil should form a government?

D.M.: I suppose you're joking? That crowd is all mad. But they done all right out of their madness.

I.M.: Perhaps then a coalition of all parties under the leadership of de Valera?

D.M. (*look of blank inquiry*): Who? Say that AGAIN.

I.M.: De Valera . . .

D.M.: Dev . . . a . . . lera? You mean the fellow that went to America? But shure me dear man that fellow's as mad as a hatter.

I.M.: Maybe the country might for a change try a Labour government, with Bill Norton at the helm.

D.M. (*gesture of holy resignation*): I met all that Labour crowd in the old days. I seen them, I built suits on their fathers. I seen them marching and counter-marching before you were born. And I'll tell you one thing about that crowd. They're no damn good to anybody. Nor never was any good to anybody.

I.M. (*smiling*): Well, how about Peadar forming a government?

D.M. (*suspiciously*): Which of the Peadars? Doyle or Cowan?

I.M.: Oh . . . either.

D.M.: I will tell you what I would do with that pair, I would tie the two of them into the one good big sack and put them into the Liffey at high tide and it would be good riddance to bad rubbish, now do you understand me?

I.M.: I see . . . Tell me, what will you have?

D.M. (*look of sourness, reluctance, disdain, replaced by one of resignation*): Oh . . . the same, I suppose.

NOTE: That is all, I suppose I need record—except perhaps to mention that frugal I.M. was astonished to find that a small quantity of cider costs three shillings and that it is customary to lace it with a baby bottle of soda water, value 4d.

Controversy, Debate

Not the least of my duties is keeping an eye on the Editor of this newspaper and rebutting, for the benefit of our simpler readers, the various heresies propounded in his leading articles. Saturday's article was a great shock to me.

It amounted to this: *The Irish Times* is four-square behind the theory newly put out by certain statesmen that we must all work harder, produce more, pay heavier taxes, endure austerities, increase our exports and reduce our imports.

I do not denounce this theory as false, but I do say that the thinking back of it is fallacious and incomplete, and that the 'economic' reasoning which begat it is obsolete.

There is postulated an equation: production = consumption; or, if you prefer it, exports = imports.

What rubbish! You don't believe me? Then ask Dr Schacht. He ran a world war on the negation of it.

There is no intrinsic distinction between the economic and financial status of the individual and the State of which he is a member. If the State must 'pay its way', so must the individuals constituting it. How many individuals do? Hardly any at all. It was reported in the papers the other day that some fellow earning £20 a week had applied for the tenancy of a subsidised house erected by the Dublin Corporation. In any modern community, nearly, there is a tiny coterie of individuals who work very hard and produce a considerable surplus. The great mass of the rest consume the surplus. Even that most highly organised lodge, the beehive, exemplifies this principle—and the bees can even claim that they have unaidedly made their own mess without reading volumes of twaddle written by fellows like Keynes, Laski or Gregory. They don't read even the *Statist*, the thinking man's comic-cuts. At the present time the U.S. has a vast surplus which is being doled out whether under the guise of 'grant' or 'loan', all over the world, even into Iron Curtain countries. The

survival of the U.S. itself depends on this policy. Hearken to
our Editor:

Ever since the foundation of the Irish State this newspaper has
been preaching the doctrine of retrenchment. Basically, Ireland is
a poor country. Virtually its only raw material is the soil, to the
efficient productivity of which there are very definite limits. Yet
our people insist that they shall enjoy living standards as high as
those of some of the richest countries in the world.

Which, I wonder, are the richest countries in the world?
Britain—where eating is practically illegal? Latin countries,
such as Spain, France, Italy, the Argentine, in which the
stark poverty of the peasantry has become an ineradicable
tradition? Russia? India? Red China?

The Editor asserts that virtually our only raw material is
the soil. Largely true. And what have we been doing with it?
Steadily exporting the best of it in large brown lumps known
as cattle. With that subject I dealt at length some years ago,
and anybody interested in soil erosion will find good books
on the subject in most libraries. The direct result is the great
new crop of hospitals and medical palaces, hordes of doctors
going up and down the country trying to do something about
bad eyesight, rotten teeth, tuberculosis, cancer, and the rest
of today's ghastly heritage. For people, too, come from the
soil.

Retrenchment? Work harder? For what?

To import more tea to make us still more neurotic, more
tobacco to poison us, more vast vulgar American motor cars
to kill more people on roads never designed for them? Is that
it? More brandy? More newsprint wherewith to disseminate
more chauvin rubbish?

This country is already enough of a laugh. We have in this
country a 'Central Bank' dominated by aliens who see to it
that our bank notes—the sterling notes with the harps and
shamrocks—are printed in Britain. I saw in the paper the
other day a picture containing members of our Central Bank,
obviously bulging with pride, present at a ceremony concerned with the installation in Dublin (by aliens) of machinery to print bank notes for Pakistan.

Seán T. is the best of fellows, but I think he is due to retire next year. It is almost certain that somewhere in Germany or Holland there is to be found a gentleman with the name of Hans Andersen. Could we not find him and make him our next President?

Wouldn't he be the right man for Fairland?

Today, undismayed by many a reverse, I take up the cudgels on behalf of the Irish nation against the historic enemy of the Irish nation—the Editor of *The Irish Times*.

(Did you ever see me cudgels? I can tell you that they are pretty hefty articles, particularly if you get them on the head!)

I suppose the reader saw yesterday's leading article?

It was concerned with this great heresy—that you must export or die.

Import implies *export*!

By a coincidence, the contrary is also true.

You can't import without exporting. Why import at all— or why not live here as Providence intended?

The complete answer to this riddle was given by me here weeks ago.

Let us depress our standard of living. Let ourselves cough less in the morning from smaller doses of Californian tobacco. Let our wives suffer less from the intoxication of tea. It will be a terrible blow, but let us try to manage without the monstrous American motorcars.

Those thoughts were provoked by our thoughtful Editor who, yesterday, expressed momentous concern at the notion that a trade union concerned with seamen might go on strike.

Anything better for the country and its sane-thinking citizens I cannot imagine.

Now for a change I am going to be serious—though only temporarily. Certain 'experts', statisticians and the like, habitually make public complaint about emigration, which is a handy word describing the atmosphere of this unfortunate country.

The real complaint is this—the true trouble-makers *don't* emigrate, and stay at home, spending their lives as scolds in newspapers (like this one, though I write from New York).

Is there any chance of getting our Government experts to

get the hell out of here and leave us alone to till our patches of potatoes and our banks of turf? Any chance of getting the E.C.A. impostors out?

I don't think the present crowd is any different from th'other crowd.

This newspaper recently revealed, as the authorised organ of a food-producing country, that a sandwich costs one shilling and fourpence in Harecourt Street Station in Dublin.

Why is nothing done about such outrages?

In the old days I used to go into Trinity College for me lunch. A very big meal cost me one and sixpence. I suppose the same meal costs one and ninepence now, but that extra thruppence is ample material to use as ammunition against the Masons.

I am no crank.

(*Take that smirk off yer face, reader!*) I mean exactly what I say.

I see little chance of beating the English out of Ireland, no chance at all of eliminating their imperial notions of trade and finance.

But I have a new idea. What are the chances of beating the Irish out of Ireland?

It's a difficult business. British Railways may seem merely inept in their mailboat policy, but it is really aimed at keeping the Irish in Ireland.

With great ferocity, I say that that is plain cheating.

Our constitutional right to be a nuisance all over the earth is indefeasible. The man who doubts that proposition takes his life in his hands and will reckon with me.

A newspaper report informs me that my old friend and former colleague, the Very Rev. Doctor Lucey, has been lecturing on the subject of 'Towards a Living Wage for Irish Workers'. Indeed, it is a subject after my own heart. (You doubt me? *Num igitur censes, ullum animal, quod sanguinem habeat sine corde esse posset?* Considering that the heart is a machine for pumping blood, I characterise Cicero's ancient query as a silly sneer at me, an expression of his own jealousy.)

Doctor Lucey appears to have stated as facts a number of propositions which are debatable. 'We were pushing out our people and losing them to England,' the report says. 'We were dying as a nation. If we are to stop emigration, we must find the reason, and part of it is that we have not the work, or, at any rate, work at a wage corresponding to what people get in other countries . . .'

In the first place, permit me to observe that nations do not die by dispersal. A nation is not necessarily a territorial agglomeration. Nations usually express their existence—here I am indebted to the news columns of the *Daily Mail*—by the domestic manufacture of bombs, by secret cellular organisation, by the possession of 'dumps', and, above all, by hostility to the British. The most pronounced nation, at the moment of going to press, is the Jewish nation. Here be it placed on record that I admire the Jews for their tenacity, resource and technical skill in meeting the military might of London oil companies. Dr Lucey does not appear to realise that Jews are merely supra-national Irishmen or, conversely, that Irishmen are land-inhibited Jews.

Let me put it another way, as Bobby Jones once remarked to me in Delgany. There is nothing wrong with emigration *per se*. It looks bad and it causes a pang; when the eldest boy left the house to get married (at the age of forty-eight) everybody was sorry and the sisters cried a bit, but it was a healthy gesture intrinsically. Ireland is not a nation in the morbid sense that England is a nation—i.e. a vast concourse of ladies and gentlemen with yellow complexions subsisting on imported offals in conditions of chronic overcrowding in an insular hereditament unfit for human habitation. The better Irish type conceives its historic environs to be the entire globe, its native island being in the nature of an incubator: 'From the national point of view of getting our people to remain at home,' says Dr Lucey, 'we must improve their conditions.' That remark entirely begs the question of whether our people should remain at home at all. Why should they? Suppose they all *do* stay at home? Who is going to beat up nigger republics, flog the copper backs of Asiatic malcontents, scourge the Indian on his native heath? Is there a presumption that the spot upon which a person is born, being that person's home, is mystically endowed with genial properties not possessed by the municipality of Shanghai? By the Police Department, City of Boston, Mass.? Is the speaking of Irish . . . illegal, outside Ireland?

Ah no, I'm afraid that view isn't very profound. I have discussed this matter several times with Irish peasants in the lounge of the Gresham. They all wore double-breasted jackets with very wide lapels, platinum wrist-watches and they smoked cigars. They gave me to understand that they pitied all Irish exiles. Know where the exiles are? *In Ireland!* Just think that over! An Irish exile is one cut off from the grandeur and the opportunity of continental life, highly bred animals unentered for the bigger and worthwhile races. The best Irishmen go abroad because they do not like the national wallpaper; the weakling residue remains at home and tries to get into the Dublin Corporation. That's why life in Ireland is so chronically unsatisfactory. You don't cure a situation like that by an expedient such as paying a 'living wage'. Next Monday I intend to give a long, boring, and superior lecture on the many other blunders made by Dr Lucey in his discourse.

A number of readers have written asking me for definitive adjudication on the Mother and Child row. This invitation I must decline—for two reasons. I deny that I am a child and I can *prove* I am not a mother.

More betoken, my interest in most things lies in the nominal rather than the phenomenal aspect. Some fine day I intend to try to get to the bottom of WHAT'S GOING ON HERE— the real world here, rather than the world of seeming. Are we all liars and humbugs and if so, why not? Are we national exemplars of Vico's theory of ultimate chaos? Or is it our simple alibi that we have a few halves in us and prefer to air our views rather than view our heirs? (The latter are usually asleep when we arrive home by taxi.)

I dunno. There seems to be a terrible logic in our affairs. In recent weeks our newspapers have been packed with pronouncements from the Irish Medical Association on moral, ethical and philosophic themes, with never a mention of MONEY anywhere; yesterday we read the report of the conclusion of the coroner's inquest on a man who died apparently as a result of a squabble among doctors.

'Nichevo' recorded last Saturday that the Editor of this paper was denounced in the *Standard* (a small pious weekly taken by the innocent to be the voice of the Catholic Church and as such profitably sold at church doors) as a 'megalomaniac journalist'. The phrase interested me. What nature of man can this be, I asked myself, who so effortlessly avoids the correct word 'megalomanic'? I bought the *Standard* and find he is none other than Alfred O'Rahilly, M.A., D.Sc., formally described as 'President, University College, Cork'.

I have read his stuff. It is a tirade saturated with insolence, arrogance and ignorance. An M.A., by Gob? I, too, am an M.A. of the same wretched university and can prove documentarily (by producing the preposterous 'thesis') that the degree, like the university, is a fake. There is, however, nothing fake about being president of any of its colleges.

But let's not be too serious. O'Rahilly is a self-licensed demagogue. Most demagogues are bores, usually because they have only one hobby-horse. O'Rahilly is not a bore for the reason that he has more hobby-horses in his stable than even myself (monstrous assertion!). A fact, lads! He is chemist, theologian, economist, authority on pig-rearing, sociologist, authority on medical jurisprudence, journalist, gentleman—goodness knows what else. He resembles my own Excellency very closely, but has less money, less delicacy, smaller taste, more diminutive learning, and does not drink whiskey. The latter point is awfully important. If he had a few drinks for himself (there's a damn good little place down there beyant called the Oyster Tavern), he would see the absurdity of his idea that the Catholic Church in this country is in danger and in need of his protection, and that this protection must be afforded by something next-door to foul-mouthedness. The Church would not be the first institution or person to be embarrassed by the solicitous concern of friends.

In his stuff in the *Standard*, the Professor purports to roast the Editor of this paper for the queer reason that the latter has been guilty of certain 'scoldings'. Here we have a matter of burning public interest; *The Irish Times*, having taken up an attitude, permissible but apparently hostile to general public thinking, throws its correspondence open to all, and publishes many letters in defence of the bishops. What does the Professor say? 'The other papers,' he says, 'so far as I have seen them, have taken refuge in grim silence.' If this paper also said nothing, I suppose the silence would be described as 'sinister'.

Read the following numbered extracts from O'Rahilly's treatise:

(1) *Unfortunately, the enforced resignation of Dr Browne has been accompanied by a flood of vituperation and an indecent public washing of dirty linen.*

I have no desire to exacerbate the feelings aroused or to adopt an attitude of partisanship. My object is to refute hostile misrepresentations and to vindicate certain important principles which have emerged from the incident.

(2) The *Irish Times*, true to its tradition of episcopophagy, exploited the occasion to the full.

(3) What is much worse is to find that this self-appointed lay archbishop of Dublin is calmly assuming a social principle of his own, which, if accepted, would lead to the most abominable totalitarian tyranny, the suppression of all institutional criticism of government. For, make no mistake about it, this is the underlying assumption of *The Irish Times*.

(4) Naturally, owing to the statistical fact that Catholics are in a large majority, the Catholic bishops, in matters of faith and morals, have a decisive influence. But their claim to record ethical criticisms, in public or in private, concerning Government measures, is one which is equally applicable to religious minorities; and indeed it is even a more vital liberty for them.

The issue involved is the right of citizens, through their religious associations to pass moral judgment on the State.

It is not only childishly futile, it is actually suicidal, for a Protestant organ such as The Irish Times, *to launch an attack on this right. For its denial is plain totalitarianism.*

(5) Except for those who openly avow such monopolistic tyranny, it is illogical and even intolerable that a small clique of journalists and Leftists should deny the right of

our Catholic bishops to pass an ethical-social verdict on legislation.

(6) We have arrived at the utterly nonsensical position that *The Irish Times* claims the right to subject the Government to a daily barrage of schoolmasterish scolding, while denying to the Catholic Episcopate the right to an occasional restrained intervention purely on matters of principle. How very stupid and short-sighted is this policy!

(7) So determined is *The Irish Times* to reduce bishops to the status of silent pariahs, that, in immediate juxtaposition with the account of the Browne affair, it inserted an item under a prominent heading: 'British Commission's Plan Condemned by Bishops.' It has become a phobia with the Editor: Who will rid me of these turbulent bishops?

(8) On what grounds does *The Irish Times*, ranging beyond its own little domain, object to it? Would it equally object if the Church of England made a similar stand against the invasion of the family by the State?

(9) Beyond general supervision as regards qualifications of teachers and suitability of premises, the State has no control whatever over the teaching in national or private schools.

(10) We don't get anything for nothing. Not only is there usually exacted regimentation with loss of liberty, but, ultimately, all goods and services must, by direct or indirect taxation, be provided by the community itself.

(11) What a disgraceful mess has been made of the whole affair, floods of nasty vituperation on the one hand and cowardly silence on the other, instead of reasoned discussion.

(12) It is the right of individual and corporate criticism of Government. This is a right which vitally concerns our Protestant fellow citizens, for whom *The Irish Times* professes to cater and whom it has scurvily served.

(13) Have we no remedy but to betake ourselves to Westmoreland Street, and implore Mr Smyllie to be our mouthpiece? Such appears to be the ultimate ideal of this megalomaniac journalist, to whose smart shallowness and irrational nonsense I have now devoted sufficient space.

A few words of comment on that lot:

(1) Very funny, your man's horror of vituperation. Who dirtied that linen, anyway?

(2) I have often heard a man say, 'I'm so hungry I could eat a dead Christian Brother.' Eating bishops is a new one. I am reminded of the anecdote concerning a crash in England of cars driven by a Protestant and a Catholic clergyman respectively. 'If it wasn't for your cloth, sir,' the Protestant roared, 'I would horsewhip you.' The priest, a Tipperaryman, glared at him. 'I'd ate the head of you,' he said, 'only it's Friday.'

(3) It is worse to be a self-appointed lay Supreme Pontiff. There is already one 'Pope' in Cork, anyway.

(4) But *The Irish Times* must shut up. Shutting up independent newspapers is as commonplace as the first move of the totalitarianism. Hi, there, *La Prensa*!

(5) Yes. Those who do not agree with you instantly become 'a small clique of journalists and Leftists'. I heard it before. Ireland's Protestant Tory organ being dubbed 'Leftist' is a pretty good crack.

(6) I will lay down my life in defence of the right to scold. There I and O'Rahilly appear to agree.

(7) No silent pariah I.

(8) It's not a little domain. It is a big one and requires courage to farm it.

(9) This statement is plain false. The State trains teachers, inspects them, prescribes courses, authorises text books. I have never heard the clerical managers assailed for 'compulsory Irish'. In operating the present system the State is cute and can wash its hands when complaints are made about dirty, insanitary and unheated schools.

(10) Here is a gem of original thinking. It's a great thing to be a university man, there's no living doubt.

(11) Quite.

(12) Quite, again.

(13) Will you for goodness sake shut up, you wee Cork nuisance—unless you can expound for us what is the opposite of 'irrational nonsense'.

My own real view?

The Editor, in writing the leading article in question, lacked prudence.

The bishops, making a perfectly legitimate intervention on a vital matter, should have done so overtly, if only for the benefit of the faithful. Lenten Pastorals are obvious occasions for the enunciation of their views. In failing therein, they lacked prudence.

Melius locutus est.

(TECHNICAL NOTE: Who would you think actually prints the monstrous calumnies on the Editor of *The Irish Times* appearing in the *Standard*?

Why, The Irish Times, Ltd.

NOW who's broad-minded?)

Today I mount my roastrum (stet) to deal with Alfred O'Rahilly, the Cork *thooleramawn*, and the monstrous attack he made on my fair mane in last week's *Standard*. Many of us are getting a bit fed up with disorders fomented by these Jesuit types such as James Joyce and O'Rahilly. It must, and shall stop.

The article in question is a farrago of scurrility, falsehood, ignorance and illiterate writing. It's shockin' stuff but day by day I intend to quote every word of it here, subjecting it to extended and pitiless exegesis. If he squeals louder after this chastisement than he did after the last, he will have good reason to, for it is mostly his own cane I shall use on him.

But first, we have a slight problem. What shall we call the *gorsoon?* He mentions my own name 'which', he adds, 'I shall abbreviate into "MC" '.[1] Fair enough. These letters usually stand for Master of Ceremonies or denote the Military Cross, a decoration conferred only on persons who have displayed conspicuous valour. But he must be crazy if he expects me to use the name and style which he claims for himself, which is no less than 'Dr Alfred O'Rahilly, M.A., D.Sc., President, University College, Cork'. Obviously a mouthful like that is quite out of the question. Note in passing that the sage is a

---

[1] There is a pervasive *varia lectio* in the text. I am sometimes 'MC.', sometimes 'M.C.'. It is presumably deliberate, and therefore sinister. The latter version probably suggests that I sustain two full pints.

doctor at both ends, which is a most unusual distinction. The thing looks to me like a train with an engine at both ends, each pulling in the opposite direction. Or it's like saying that our little land is an *insula doctorum et doctorum*. Or perhaps it looks mainly like plain conceited damn nonsense.

I was reading *Kubla Khan* in the library of the dower house in Santry Great Park the other evening and the thought came to me that we might call the Doctor merely Alph the Sacred Raver. He might take offence at that, though. Phwat's wrong with his initials now—AOR? It's a perfectly straightforward Irish word, which Dinneen says means 'a personal attack in prose or verse: a curse'. So be it.

With that settled, let us now to work.

The very first thing in AOR's essay is a heading, thus:

'THE HIRED HUMORIST'

The reference is to the present Excellency. The important word is 'HIRED', intended as a sneer. AOR, skilled sociologist, is horrified and disgusted at the idea of anybody working *for money*. I think that's a most unsound attitude. Shure, me dear man, even the bishops are not above taking money. Dammit, I'll go farther and say this—AOR himself . . . (I can hardly get this monstrous slander out!) . . . *AOR himself takes money!* Truth to tell, he does not do too badly for himself at all, quartered on the backs of the taxpayers with a fat post in a university which virtually confines its public pronouncements to demands for more and more dough the more cosily to cock up its 'professors'. And would AOR, I wonder, be above squeezing five guineas a time out of poor Peter Curry, the *Standard* editor, for rubbish such as that with which I now deal? Could it be that he is hired? If I know my Corkman, I think the answer must be yes. 'The unemployed?' a man once said to me, '*That crowd?* Sure that crowd wouldn't work if you paid them.' That general attitude does not accord with *Rerum Novarum*. I am too wealthy to have any personal interest in such questions, but I formally deny that hired or otherwise, I am a 'humorist'. I am a most serious and thoughtful commentator, and a large number of persons and interests have found much of what I have written far from funny. Ask any motor assembler. I am also suave, a delightful raconteur and, generally, one of the decentest men in the whole world. The funny man in the present situation is AOR. I now quote the first two paragraphs of his spiel:

I summarily repeat this egregious editorial; for it has not been withdrawn; it has, in fact, been aggravated by being made the prelude to a continued outburst of bigotry and misrepresentation. The Editor himself seems to have been suddenly struck with aphasia, when he found himself in the unpleasant predicament of either having to withdraw his offensive leader or else attempting to answer my arguments.

Unwilling to accept either of these alternatives, he nevertheless feels that he must do something about it. So he avails himself of the services of his hired humorist, a Catholic who masquerades under the pseudonym of 'Myles na gCopaleen' (which I shall abbreviate into 'MC').

In connection with the contents of the second paragraph above, the Cork mahatma adds this much elsewhere:

I am more than disappointed that the Editor (instead of replying) has got his professional jester to emit a stream of irrelevant and stupid personal invective.

It is necessary to state that the foregoing is a falsehood. He states without qualification as a fact something upon which he has not, nor can he have, any information whatsoever. It is at least three months since I had any contact with the Editor of this newspaper. The solitary intervention he has made in this transaction was to excise from my original discourse (unjustifiably in my opinion) a passage which dealt with the labyrinth of intrigue and backstairs work[2] which is involved in appointments to university posts.

AOR does not know the meaning of the word 'egregious'. I should like him to know that it comes to us from L. *grex*, meaning 'flock', connotes a strayed sheep, and would in AOR's context mean that the editorial in question was

---

[2] But don't be talking. The chair of Irish in U.C.D. is vacant and reports of the events pertaining to the filling thereof, which reach me almost daily, are absolutely incredible. The U.C.D. authorities will be horrified to learn that this child is in possession of the document issued by the Arts Faculty and feth, he'll prent it!

entirely unusual, utterly alien to the 'form' of this newspaper. It was, of course, entirely characteristic of the paper.

I will say nothing of the eccentric feat, attributed to my Eminence of masquerading under a pseudonym, but would draw attention to the Editor's plight, i.e. being suddenly struck with aphasia. In his preceding drool, AOR kindly gave us the word 'episcopophagy'. There is certainly nothing like the education, matteradamn what you say it was never a burden to any man. (I will tell you another man that was very nearly struck with half Asia—MacArthur!)

I continue my funny discourse tomorrow.

Did you read me yesterday on Alfred O'Rahilly, the Cork *gawskogue*? I was damn funny, if I say it myself. It was right gas. But I overlooked one small comment I had intended. AOR referred to me as 'a Catholic who masquerades under the pseudonym of "Myles na gCopaleen" '. Thanks, but why this perfectly gratuitous assertion that I am a Catholic? How does AOR know what my beliefs are, or what nature is my creed? I do not lightly take on the grandiose title of Catholic. If AOR is a Catholic, it follows that I am not: the contrary would suggest the equation AOR = MC which is perfectly preposterous. In any event, I deny absolutely that I am an Irish Catholic; dub me that and you dub me heresiarch.

I promised to quote AOR's drool paragraph by paragraph and having managed to deal with two of them yesterday, I now reach the third. This:

Ordinarily I would take no notice of a writer who with studied buffoonery divagates into paltry trivialities and offensive epithets as a subterfuge from a sociological discussion for which he is incompetent. But he asserts: 'A number of readers have written asking me for definitive adjudication.' If we may judge by some of the correspondents of *The Irish Times*, this ridiculous exaltation of MC into a super-bishop may well be true. Anyway, several people have taken the matter seriously and have written to me. So in the absence of any editorial reply, I will deal briefly with the Editor's blustering substitute.

When a thing is intrinsically funny, it is possible to spoil it by comment. However, we'll chance it.

Number wan, I really don't think it necessary to describe

'trivialities' as being 'paltry'. I never heard of a momentous triviality. But where are we at all, at all, when the Crok philosopher (stet), ridiculing the idea of people writing to my Excellency for advice on spiritual matters, immediately asserts that 'several people' have written to himself? I wonder would they be the same people? 'Me dear Doctor, I was on to Myles but could get nothing out of him at all only studied buffoonery divigating into paltry trivialities. Please let me know is the bishops all gone mad . . .'

Number two: Wot's all this about the exaltation of myself into a super-bishop? It's a crack that comes well from AOR, who describes himself as 'President, University College, Cork'. My Greek dictionary states quite bluntly that the word *episkopos* means 'president'. Really, I have no ecclesiastical ambitions and I was never a member of the Jesuits: I am merely a spoiled Proust. BUT—and this is awfully important—AOR should be aware that the Catholic Church does not require that one should be a clergyman, of however low degree, to be made a cardinal. Suppose—just *suppose* for a minit—that the Red Hat should go, not to Drumcondra or Ardmagh, but to Santry! That would certainly shake some people. 'No, sir, he's not in. Matterafact, he's across in Rome.' By Gob, stranger things have happened. I wonder would AOR muster sufficient humility to kneel devoutly and kiss my ring? However . . .

I showed yesterday that AOR uttered a falsehood when he asserted that the Editor of this paper, afraid to make any move himself from his editorial eyrie, covertly prevailed upon myself to give AOR a public hiding. Now read again the tail-end of the quotation above. I am awarded the title of 'Editor's blustering substitute'. In the same issue of the *Standard*, the editorial article is concerned with the important subject of money. The editor of the paper having published a full-page advertisement crying the merits of Dr Browne's apparently godless Mother and Child scheme, thought it better to pipe down till the bad smell subsided. And so, 'in the absence of any editorial reply', as AOR says, it is he who will deal with me. He says himself that, so far as the *Standard* is concerned, he is 'the Editor's blustering substitute'. Or has the unfortunate chiner's prose broken down again?

But the really funny word in the tail-end of the paragraph is 'briefly'. The Corker's idea of brevity is of the same order as his veracity, his learning, his reasoning powers and even his syntax: namely: less than mediocre. He deals with me briefly in some three full columns, all of which I will quote here. That means that his brevity may keep us all here till Christmas.

I pass to the next paragraph which is headed 'Gems of Invective'. The suggestion behind *that* is that I live in a glass house and therefore shouldn't throw precious stones. Read it yourself:

In a matter involving such far-reaching issues, especially when the campaign was opened so offensively, I have no objection to good hard-hitting argumentation. The Editor of *The Irish Times* is unknown to me; I have reason to believe that he is personally a liberal, fair-minded gentleman. But I am concerned only with him as a journalist. For all I know he may have written with his tongue in his cheek, to play up to the gallery, or to increase the circulation of his paper by a *succès de scandale*.

I have vigorously argued against his editorial; I am disappointed that he has not replied with equal vigour. I am more than disappointed that, instead of this, he has got his professional jester to emit a stream of irrelevant and stupid personal invective.

Honest, lads—isn't he the most extraordinary and incorrigible *thullabawn?* The 'blustering substitute' becomes the 'professional jester', changes his clothes lower down in AOR's treatise and becomes a 'phraseological gunman', later is stated to own a 'jester's cap and bells' and still later becomes a 'pseudonymous jester' who emits 'vulgar cat-calls'. (By the way, I wonder whether a cat-call could in certain circumstances, be felicitous?)

More particularly I wonder what is the nature of the reason AOR says he has for believing that the Editor of this newspaper is 'a liberal, fair-minded gentleman'. AOR must be confusing the Editor with myself. The Editor is nothing of the kind. He is a bigot who has sufficient intelligence to propagate his bigotry with a show of humanism and broadmindedness. He has many of the characteristics of AOR himself, though he cannot match him either in stupidity or in his personal consate of hisself.

Naturally, all such judgments and comparisons are relative. In this part of the world the norm is I ('is I' sounds a bit pedantic, I admit). In my only can you descry the statutory and sapient 4840 square yards.[3]

As you read this, I am writing some extremely amusing stuff, replete with quotations from AOR's drool, for tomorrow. I never knuwn meself in better form!

Yesterday morning I received by registered post a parcel containing chocolates having liqueur centres. Under my microscope each showed evidence of tiny punctures such as would be made by a hypodermic needle. The postmark was 'CORCAIGH'. I put the lot in the fire.

I now resume my excurses (stet) on the treatise which Alfred O'Rahilly published in the *Standard* on the subject of myself. O'Rahilly's forebear, Sir Walter O'Rahilly, is credited with having brought the potato to Ireland. I am sure by now that Sir Alfred O'Raleigh realises that he has achieved the superior feat of laying an egg. Permit me to proceed to the next quotation from his work:

It is sufficient for me to record without comment a few specimens of the language used towards me by M.C.:

'*Insolence, arrogance and ignorance*'
'*A self-licensed demagogue*'
'*An authority on pig-rearing*'
'*You wee Cork nuisance*'

But who am I to object? In this paper (March 26th 1943), the well-known drama critic, Gabriel Fallon, objected to the expletives, nitwit phrases and nasty dirt of MC's adaptation of a play by Capek. In the issue for 2nd April MC calls Mr Fallon a 'wretched pedant' and says: 'That your Mr Fallon is not even educated is evident from the extraordinary stuff he publishes in your paper every week.' So Mr Fallon and myself are branded as contributors to 'a small pious weekly'—which has about twice the circulation of *The Irish Times*.

On rereading this stuff, I am almost sorry that I have noticed this incoherent ranter. But I do so firstly to express my surprise that *The Irish Times* should publish such ill-mannered abuse, and

[3] I am a wiseacre.

secondly to show up the Editor's unworthy attempt to avoid argument by enlisting the aid of his phraseological gunman.

I will now take the class slowly through that.

I do not quite understand what AOR means by the phrase 'without comment'. The remainder of the quotation (and the various other extracts I have shown) look to me suspiciously like comment.

Nor can I understand the setting by AOR of my accurate descriptions of him in a context of hysterical abuse. The fact of the matter is that we find him at his dinner. (He is getting his ragout!) He demonstrates in that very quotation (as well as *passim* in his treatease) that he is insolent, arrogant and ignorant. He calls me a ranter, for instance. Actually I am a *rentier*—an entirely different matter. For his own part, he will not deny that he is a demagogue. Self-licensed? Surely to the sacred godfathers he is not suggesting that anybody else has licensed him. I will raise holy melia murder if I find that the Most Reverend Dr Cohalan has issued a licence to him, and if such licence exists, I will have it endorsed and suspended immediately.

Does AOR deny that he is an authority on pig-rearing, or that he has ever set himself forth as an authority on agricultural? If so, I withdraw, but cannot see how one can increase one's stature by denying all knowledge of an important and technical matter. He *may* deny, until he is purple in the face, that he is a nuisance but I aver that he will find absolutely nobody else to share so outlandish a theory. He may deny that he is wee, but wee he is: he stands five feet four inches in his socks. I *know* that, because I measured him once from a distance, by triangulation. And not even he will have the cheek to deny that he is 'Cork'. No, I fear my definitions are accurate.

Wot's all this about Mr Fallon? Is it an invitation that he should fall on me again? I hope not. Mr Fallon is a good, neat, tidy little man. Nothing will induce me not even a taunt from AOR, to attack such a man. The year 1943 is a bit far off. In the intervening eight years Mr Fallon has had the inestimable advantage of reading my notes in this newspaper, and is now probably highly educated. I wonder would he favourably review that new play I am writing—*The Shadow of a Phraseological Gunman?* I hope so.

I am very surprised that AOR, who claims elsewhere to have an English dictionary, has absolutely no idea of the meaning of the word 'dirt'. Etymologically, the word is very nasty, but no literate person may refer in my presence to 'nasty dirt'.

I called the *Standard* a small, pious weekly. This enrages AOR. Why? It *is* small, it *is* pious and it *is* a weekly. AOR says its circulation (which nobody mentioned) is 'about twice' that of this newspaper. That's a good wan certainly. I have never met any living soul who knows what the circulation of *The Irish Times* is, even approximately. I really believe NOBODY knows and have been told that the customary enumerating device is missing from the printing presses. AOR has not one shred of justification for his statement which, as usual, is presented as an ascertained fact.

I solemnly warn readers that we are as yet, after three days, only on the fringe of the *silva orahilla*. Grievous and arduous days lie ahead. One of them is tomorrow, Saturday, and we *may* get a special edition out to keep the ball rolling over Sunday. We'll see.

Today I continue my discourse on Alfred O'Rahilly, the Cork fellow and lexicophagor. My next quotation is this:

It is difficult in all this chaff to discover a grain of relevant argument. Here is the only one I can find. Under the delusion that our national schools were 'State schools', Dr Browne quoted the parallel of compulsory primary education as justifying his scheme. The Bishops briefly alluded to this assertion as a 'fallacy', and I developed the point. I showed that constitutionally the national schools were family schools, and that the parents could use any other schools; or could themselves educate their children.

With that metropolitan smugness so characteristic of some of our civil servants, it is assumed that I, who have spent my life at education, am ignorant of the fact that the State approves texts and, at least on paper, forbids religious emblems. This is, of course, a hangover from the British régime, and is tolerated as a fact and not as a right. Several years ago I wrote at length on this subject in this paper, and refuted the very assertion now made by M.C.

That word 'chaff' is pretty important. Wot does it mean, I
wonder? Wer's me dictionary? The book says it means '(a
corruption of *chafe*, to irritate or annoy). To assail with
sarcastic banter or raillery: to banter; to make game of . . .'

Under a different heading the book refers to the 'glumes'
of corn and grasses (would you call AOR the 'glumey
Dean'?) 'but . . . separated from the corn . . . by thrashing . . .' Any thrashing that is going on here is being performed by me.

Let nobody forget that.

In regard to the latter paragraph quoted above. I never
referred to AOR as a civil servant and certainly never accused
him of 'metropolitan' smugness. He is, of course, a civil
servant, being paid by the tolerant State. Logically, however,
this is not to say that he becomes smug. He is already smug.
He is both smug and smug and doing, in this mysterious
principality of Cork, all right for himself.

AOR's statement that he has spent 'my life at education'
interests me because it reminds me of the mad brother, who
purports to operate a medical practice in the town of
Brighton. Where is the brother, fellows ask me? Don't you
know where he is, I invariably reply, he is a doctor across in
Brighton. *They* know, as too well I know myself, that he is in
the front-drawn-room drinking MY malt. But he never com-
mits the stupid sin of becoming drunk. So long as his mouth
is not gagged by the unspeechifying glass, he accuses everybody in sight (not excluding the present Eminence) of being
drunk and making a show of themselves. *De AOR fabula
narratur.* He says that he has spent his 'life' at education but
appears before readers of this good paper as a person who has
been quite untouched by what most of us accept as education. The fact that he doesn't know what he is talking about
is posterior to the fact that he is incoherent.

Consider merely the comment cited above, to the objection
of the British Government to religious emblems, at least on
paper. I think the British is pairfictly right. As a young father
of an oldish family I got certain religious catch-cries printed
on newsprint some years ago by J. J. O'Leary, owner of
Cahill's of Parkgate Street, Dublin. In about a half an hour
the chislers had the slogans turn apart. (In King's English,

'torn apart'.) After that day's work, all my slogans are printed on either linen or canvas. Does this mean excommunication? I hope not.

I now quote AOR's next paragraph:

'*This statement is plain (sic) false. The State trains teachers, inspects them, prescribes courses, authorises textbooks.*'

The State does not train teachers, nor does it appoint or pay them. It is allowed, in fact, to prescribe textbooks for certain schools, but I have always denied its right to do so. In reply to another critic, who made the same mistake as M.C., I wrote in this paper in the issue for November 15th 1946.

I need hardly add that the word 'sic' in the above was inserted by AOR, not by me, in gratuitous proof of his unknowledge of English. The idea, if accepted, will involve public expense. Road authorities who put up a sign reading DEAD SLOW will have to change it to DEADLY SLOW in order not to offend this Cork fellow.

And poor General Mulcahy? God knows he has enough to answer for but the suggestion that he is running away with millions of pounds, to his Department annually voted by Parliament, is most unworthy. For all I know it may be true that the State does not train teachers. I wouldn't mind a paltry sixty-three thousand pounds in the current Estimates volume dedicated officially to 'Training of Teachers'. But when, in the same book, I see that five and a half million pounds of public money is voted for 'salaries, etc.' of teachers, I am forced to the opinion that either the State pays national teachers or else Mulcahy should be behind bars. (An I'll settle for the first guess.) I think AOR is very cruel to reveal so late in the day that the national teachers, who went on strike for more pay and camped pickets on the steps of the Minister's office, should have instead harassed the house of the local P.P.

What, reader, would you think this diminutive Cork lyceum known as U.C.C. costs YOU?

Why, only ninety-nine thousand pounds a year.

In a way, I suppose it's all right.

In a way.

NOTE: MC devoted three further articles to AOR's second
    article in the *Standard* quoted extensively above.

The original function of architecture was not housing people but the material expression of political authority. Apart from intact examples of this, such as Athens, Rome and the centre of London, one has the architectural remains of older civilisations, such as the Inca and the Egyptian; they all show a two-class society composed of masters and slaves, the masters using grandiose public buildings as convenient manifestations of might. The Church in time also adopted this magistral symbolism. When with the formation of the middle classes society became three-class, traders and various other groups joined the State and Church in making, by architectural gestures, affirmations of self-esteem and power. This architecture came to connote the expression of contemporary prosperities and, generally speaking, to reflect the moral and psychological condition of society.

Now here is the important point. When that society sickened, its sickness was instantly reflected in contemporary architecture; not only reflected, but underlined, exaggerated and helped along. Architecture became more diseased than its context and itself became a force further disrupting society, assailing public morality and taste. When through political upheaval society is subjected to conditions of chaos, the true function of architecture is to reaffirm the idea of continuity and dignity, to instil coolness and to discourage orgies of emotion. After the First World War, Berlin became the world centre of social instability, vice and pernicious 'tomorrow-we-die' philosophies. All values were discarded and in architecture as well as art there began a period of cultivated decadence, vulgarity, cynicism and sensualism. With all standards and rules gone, technique or training no longer inhibited expression, and the disfigurement of public places became nearly everybody's business. And the malady spread throughout Europe and to America. What began as an aspect of social disease has now become a 'school'. Pretentiousness, flashiness, affectation, feminism, 'smartness' and general vulgarity are the characteristics of this 'school'.

Whether architecture should or should not express or reflect bad and good social trends is an academic biological conundrum: it is sufficient to note that in many places it has and does, BUT ... here is a far simpler question: Should architecture express troubles, unrests and social neuroses *which don't exist?* One can answer yes provided one approves highly of perversion, humbug, vulgarity, stupidity, ignorance and the talent of inferior mammals to ape and copy without understanding.

For that is just what is happening in Ireland. Here we have the patient and medicine bottles without the disease. The profound intellectual, ideological and social cataclysms which rack this country are being 'expressed' by young architects in such time as they can spare between the four solid meals a day. One is familiar with the simple-minded person who gets hold of a medical textbook and straightway discovers that he is simultaneously suffering from twelve or fifteen diseases, all fatal. It is nothing to what happens to the young solid middle-class Irish architect when he gets his hand on glossy American and Continental trade journals. Paranoia is no name for the state he gets into. This incredible *Year-Book* we have been discussing sent away for 'messages' from 'distinguished architects abroad'. (I have explained who *they* are.) The 'messages' duly arrived: listen to this for stuff to be put into the heads of young impressionable Irish folk:

We have now reached, in the best utilitarian and domestic building, forms at the level of a good locomotive, a good car, a good dentist-tool. Sound technical forms which in their honesty become of cultural value.

It is a beginning; not, as some architects seem to think, already an end. It is the basis for a new architecture: a notable part of its grammar, but still not very much in the way of literature. It is *good building*, but not yet *emotional building*; not yet Architecture!

You see what this means? That when you ask an Irish architect to design a house for you, you are really inviting His Nibs to express his 'emotions'—in which you and not he will have to afterwards *live*!

Indeed, it mightn't be so bad if an Irish architect did express his 'emotions', for he is nearly always a solid soul. The Irish tradition in art and architecture is cold, intellectual and formal—compare the Rock of Cashel with Cologne Cathedral. True Irish art has a monastic horror of emotion. The young Irish architect simply does not have this 'emotion'

the Continental gentleman thinks is so important. How come
that he still 'expresses' it?

Take a specific case. A highly cultivated and sensitive mid-
European whose profession is architecture loses everything
except his life and a remnant of his reason in the abomina-
tions of a Hitlerite State. His mind is affected and his emotional mechanism is in permanent riot. His architectural
work becomes the expression of nervous breakdown. He now
lives, say, in America, and he has never even heard of Ireland.

How come that one encounters this same nervous breakdown, erected in an Irish field, unbelievably stark and
violent against the soft Irish skies? Well, no matter who is
embarrassed, I fear we must be frank: it is not the same
nervous breakdown but a secondhand nervous breakdown, a
fair copy, and is the work of a terribly healthy Irish architect.
Although he has not been hit at all, he often cries more loudly
than the original sufferer. I am not clear why anybody's
nervous troubles or emotional derangements should be
recorded in public, even if they *are* rated, but I am quite
clear that the Irish city and countryside is not the best place
to perpetuate memorially the sufferings of aliens. This thing
will have to be stopped.

Normally I am content to diagnose, leaving treatment to
others, but in this instance I am prepared to make an
exception. *Provided* this Institute of Architects shows a
change of heart and undertakes to publish no more 'Year-
Books'. I am prepared to give the members a Summer
School of lectures under the following titles:

1 The importance of sincerity and personal experience.
2 It is vulgar to make a scene in public; houses must conform
  to the same standards of behaviour as people.
3 Taste: what is it?
4 The Dangers of Dabbling.
5 Der Mylsismus als Kunstbegrundung.
6 Les Folies Betjemans.
7 Manners for Architects.
8 Some aspects of the Lady Architect.
9 Can Architects play Chess?

Well, there is my offer. Could anything be fairer?

Am I, I asked myself the other day, a king's man? Basilephile or smouldering regicide, which? I instantly reminded myself of Sainte-Beuve's warning: *Ne me demandez pas ce que j'aime et ce que je crois, n'allez pas au fond de mon âme.* So I didn't ask the question again and the subject dropped. Bit of a stony silence afterwards, too. Truth to tell, I'm rather sensitive people.

But ... I do not mind hinting that this question as to whether I yield fealty to any earthly monarch involves us in certain theological *quaestiunculae*: is it my *mens* I am expected to renounce and proffer, or my *animus*, or both? The truth is that this 'loyalty', of which one hears so much in Great Northern Ireland, has never been defined. Does loyalty inhibit behaviour? If I am a king's man, am I seated in treason if I have dinner with a group of irredentist intellectuals? Can one be loyally identified with the Crown while asking naught but the society of commoners? Divilamatter what king says he owns me, I will slip into the snug in Meagher's and have a pint with the shawlies. I wrote a poem in praise of that little nook once, it goes something like this:

> This royal thing of crones, this scepter'd tile,
> This heart of majesty, this seat of Meagher's,
> This other Eden, demi-paradise,
> This blessed pot, this hearth, this room, this ingle-land ...

But ... on the broader question of 'loyalty' as a gesture of acquiescence in an aristocratic organisation of society and of the administration of immature communities by the brains of England (Churchill once called me 'a sombre and tattered lackey' but I bear no grudges) I am all in favour of it, nor have I ever scrupled to bend my niece before His Majesty King George VI. (Though where he got these Red Ministers of his from is a mystery to me, and a great sorrow also.) But with me, as assuredly it is with Mr Dillon, being loyal is a suave, mechanistical, perfectly *natural* process of assent and by no means a shrill, worried and self-conscious protestation. I say it with regret, but the latter is the condition of my Lord Dunsany. (Can it be that Dunsany is a reformed rebel?) I have full documentation, it is all there in black and white, chapter and verse can be given for every word I say. There

is, after all, such a thing as intrusive, gratuitous and irrelevant declarations of adherence to the Throne, and all such
are regarded by me with great suspicion. I am by no means
persuaded of the political stability of a German who says
'Heil Hitler, what's for breakfast?' Or take this other dialogue
in a restaurant:

WAITER: Soup, sir?
LORD DUNSANY: Where would the world be today but for
the Royal Navy?
WAITER (*taken back*): Er . . . possibly . . . hors d'oeuvres,
sir?
LORD DUNSANY: God save the King!

I cannot say whether that conversation actually took place,
of course, since I am not a waiter, but I have proof of something worse. It is a 'book review' by his Lordship which
appeared in the *Sunday Times*. It is, indeed, a very surprising
screed, and even contains an oblique reference to the book
under 'review'. I must first deal with this portion, before
emptying the vials of Moyrath on the head of his unhappy
Lordship. He observes, preliminarily:

It is a guide to Dublin . . . and usually accurate, though it is not
so where the South of Ireland is referred to as a republic, or where
we are told that a Kingfisher is to be found on the Irish farthing;
the one is part of the British Commonwealth, and the other is a
woodcock . . .

Now that is fair enough. There is a hint of petulance there
about 'republic' and 'Commonwealth', but his Lordship's
main anxiety is to deny that the Irish have been so disloyal as
to substitute the kingfisher for the king on the farthing. (All
the same, it was probably a nearthing and not a farthing.) My
only quarrel here is that his Lordship, choosing to be pedantic about fowls, failed to point out that kingfisher is the
vulgar name for the halcyon, or the *alcedo hispida*. (*Alcedo*
from the Greek *alkuon*, found in the Iliad, 9.562. Cf. also
polyphlosbos thalassa, the resounding sea, *ibid. passim.*) You
can also cf., if you like, Halcyon Hours, an animal that
would have been very *polyphlosbos* indeed, if I had got a
whip, a stick or even my boots near him, on a certain
occasion.

We now come to the incredible second half of his lordship's 'book review'. Here it is, complete and unabridged:

> Of Nelson on his great pillar he says: 'Many people wonder why
> he is allowed to remain there, now that Ireland is free.' Yet may
> one not be permitted to wonder how free Ireland would have been
> under Napoleon, if Nelson had not done as much as he did to help
> the Irishman who defeated Napoleon at Waterloo to get across the
> seas in order to do so? Indeed, were it not for the assistance that
> the Royal Navy has given in our day to Irishmen like Alexander,
> Montgomery, Gort, Dill, Alanbrooke and Auchinleck to defeat a
> modern tyranny, any freedom in Ireland would be strictly ver-
> boten.
> I recommend this book to all who would see Dublin. And, as I
> put it down, I wonder why a reviewer should not end his little
> critique as plays are ended, with the National Anthem. I will do
> so. God Save the King.

I will say nothing of the idea of anyone sneering at
Napoleon at this hour of the day, or of the unworthy gibe at
British fortitude which attributes the defeat of Hitler to
emigrant military paddies with the 'assistance' of the Royal
Navy. I would not even *know* what to say of the last paragraph
which, if it is intended as a joke, is surely a tasteless performance. My general feeling is one of deep embarrassment.
Those of us who acknowledge attachment to His Majesty
would like him to know that what we offer is adult homage
and not this Dunsany shower of broth: we do not ask to plant
on His Majesty's brow this Mick's kiss or enfold his regal
person in this voluminous Irish fair-day overcoat of weeping
slavering 'love'. What would an Englishman think of his
Lordship? He would probably raise the eyebrows and then
laugh at his Lordship but my difficulty is this—would he not
be laughing at me also? (Doesn't do, you know.)
Perhaps we had better say no more about his Lordship's
piece as a political testament. Where does it stand in the
sphere of literary criticism? As literary criticism it is trash,
and sorry trash at that, and the whole thing is a blow and a
grievous disappointment to me. I sincerely hope it will not
happen again.
Is there any reason why I should not end this 'critique'
with the National Anthem? BAH!

Parliament at present is dealing with a Bill concerning the Meath Hospital, but the Bill seems to deal mostly with legal and procedural matters. There is room for another measure to impose certain obligations in law on all hospitals, private as well as public in matters of management, not dissimilar in thought from the recent regulations seeking to ensure clean food. Though these obligations for hospitals would be uniform and universal, they would not destroy or even impair the personality of individual hospitals. For the most part they would aim at safeguarding patients, promoting efficiency and saving money.

There are certain obvious matters which need no emphasis. Patients have been killed through the use of identical couplings on cylinders containing either lethal gases or oxygen. Except for a few buckets, most hospitals have no fire-fighting equipment, no indoor hydrants; fire drill by the staff is usually unheard of.

Few if any large hospitals have an administrative head, properly paid and endowed with authority. Usually there are two boards, a Medical Board and a Board of Management. Members of the Medical Board concentrate on pursuing their technical trade—and rightly so, even if they did know anything about administration (though this is not to say that jealousy and intrigue is unknown among doctors). The Board of Management meets only at intervals to transact routine business and attempts no form of day-to-day control. Where a secretary or registrar exists, he is usually occupied with accountancy and office work, but in any event has no authority to give instructions to the various *blocs* of hospital personnel. A hospital presents more complicated problems of administration, staff control and catering than does a hotel. Yet hotels think it a good idea to have a manager.

But much smaller things interest the patient. An example:

The present Excellency spent several months in a hospital having a shattered leg attended to. The gear used in connection with this situation compels the patient to lie immovably on his back day and night for an indefinite time. It was winter, and the small ward the Excellency inhabited contained two rows of some seven beds each facing each other. At about five in the evening the lights were switched on.

They consisted of a row of blazing globes suspended along the centre of the ceiling. The patients had no option but to have these lights burning into their eyes for many hours, not only in the evening but in the early morning. An attempt to read entailed peering red-eyed at a page of print which was in complete shadow. The Excellency eventually sent out for one of those green eye-shades favoured by office workers and tennis players. It was an improvement but no cure, and did nothing about the reading problem. A bedside lamp would have helped there, but the entire ward contained only one wall plug, and another man was using that to operate a radio. Attempts at reading had to be discontinued completely, but not before the Excellency had sustained permanent damage to his sight.

The ward was cleaned twice a day—not, however, with a modern electrical appliance, but with a broom, wielded vigorously enough to ensure that the dust raised, after it had been impregnated with the different germs of different patients, was efficiently circulated all over the ward to ensure the maximum infection of everybody in general. Once a week the floor was waxed—presumably to ensure that a man recovering from a broken leg and making his first timid attempts to relearn walking, would slip and break his leg again, if not his neck.

The meals were deplorable. It did not seem that the food was bad (though some of the eggs were over two months old according to the code mark)—it was probably reasonably good food which had been put through the traditional Irish process of being botched in the kitchens by scullions who knew nothing whatever about bulk cooking. A fellow patient told me he had been in jail (I charitably assumed his had been a political offence or some noble one possibly concerned with sheltering a lady's honour) and he swore the jail diet was immensely superior. One result of this was that people who could not eat these meals began assembling private delicacies of their own such as buns, butter, chocolate and cooked ham: these they stored in their lockers, which were also the only place to store other articles such as soiled handkerchiefs, bottles of hair oil, soap and shaving tackle. Occasionally, some of these private foods were overlooked, and decomposed.

In the middle of one night the Excellency, unable to sleep, was smoking a cigarette. He noticed that the adjoining patient had suddenly started to die. The night nurse had gone off to swallow sundry cups of tea in some remote quarter and by the time she came back the man was dead. Ring the bell? There was no bell in the ward. If, startled by such a situation, I had dropped my cigarette on my own bed in some place inaccessible to me, I take it that there would have been a conflagration and the Excellency would have been incinerated. (Good enough for him, you may say—but it might be you, chum!)

Every hospital should have, of all things, a shop. Bedridden people are eternally in want of a variety of small things —tobacco, fruit, razor blades, newspapers, stamps, ink and the like, to say nothing of edible supplementary foodstuffs. Normally they have to implore ambulatory patients or nurses to get them these things when they are going out—and the latter go about loaded with hundreds of such commissions, and usually have to carry a notebook to keep track of change. The hospital shop need not amount to more than one small room, with an itinerant attendant: it will, of course (horror!), make money, either as a domestic enterprise or as a concession let to an outsider.

In some places nurses, with a job so unenviable, are treated badly, both personally and in the matter of their hours and conditions. They surely deserve the protection of the law.

But nursing itself is so arduous and absorbing that it is not reasonable to expect nursing staffs or even doctors to attend to such matters as I have mentioned above.

What is clearly requisite is a lay manager, dressed not in any authority which any Board may be pleased to concede him, but attired in the panoply of the law. An efficient hospital means the speedier recovery of the sick, briefer bed occupancy, and thus more beds.

It is as simple as that.

The modest proposal of the Amalgamated Irish Housewives and General Consorts Association, i.e. that all Irish girls over the age of twelve be forthwith shipped to the Continent as 'volunteer domestic labour' I find cold-blooded and offensive

in the extreme. I am very much in earnest about this. I am a
family, ma'am. I mean a family man. Four of the boys
(Maelscheachlann, Toirbhdhealbhach, Fionndheasmumhan
and Gealmhathghamhain) are in the Sairvice—walking ad-
vertisements for me you could call them—they are Junior
Ads to a man. The girls are all at home, of course. ('*At*,' I
said—not 'in a'!) They are not yet earning. Right. I don't
pretend that I am knocking down much in the way of wages
but I'm certainly not complaining because I have to provide
for them. True enough, the youngest girl is now twenty-
three, but the 'Irish Housewives' (Irish housewives how are
ye Moscow fly-benights disguised in shawls and petticoats
that a child could tell their real nature!!!) have another guest
(stet) coming if they think I am going to see them shanghaied
away to Hamburg in an artificial emigration wave got up for
no other purpose than to embarrass the life out of the
Government that is only doing its best. What is this slavish
passion for keeping our Irish girls not merely in domestic
service but for ever advertising to the whole world that that's
all they're fit for by actually trying to start an export trade in
them to the Continent? Sort of asthore heifers? It's not good
enough, it's the old slave complex all over again and no
amount of oul' chat or letters to the newspapers can hide that
fact from me. Gob, do you know, there was one of those
letters in the other day and it made my blood bile. This sort
of thing, if you don't mind:

> The greater number of mistresses are humane and anxious to
> treat those employed by them as they themselves would wish to be
> treated . . . I am, of course, alluding to those houses (the majority)
> where good wages, ample food, comfortable bedrooms and good
> off-duty times are given.

If the mistresses are as anxious as all that what on earth is
to stop them from doing the sensible thing that will gain them
their hearts' desire—namely going into domestic service
themselves. Surely then they will be treated by themselves as
they would wish to be treated by themselves? Are the good
mistresses aware that even in the country builders' labourers
are paid 1s 9d per hour and that they are paid this rate for
every hour worked. Is the work done by domestic servants

less arduous than that so gracefully performed by builders'
labourers, taking into account (inevitable) differences of sex
and circumstance? Assuming that a maid works only seven
hours a day—and this, of course, is not the case—how many
of them are paid four guineas a week? Is it contended that ten
shillings a week plus 'keep' amounts to anything like this
sum. And why will the Royal Irish Mistresses' Society not
permit Irish girls to take up any other profession? I have
known many Irish girls—before I was married, I nade hardly
say—and I think most readers will agree with me when I say
(which I shall any minute now—wait for it) that generally
speaking they are most superior young women mentally and
physically. I knew Ann Devlin well and little Miss Curran
above in the Priory. There was Miss G. Uaile, Miss Ni H.,
the Countess, Lady G., Miss Horniman, 'Matt' O'Hara,
Geraldine Fitzgerald, and that fascinating apostate who is
now Lady na gCopaleen (*née* Timaeri, a dusky Cypriot). And
scores of others. Nobody but a cad and a bounder would
suggest that ... our Irish women novelists for instance
should be employed at ... cooking and sairving mea-els. Am
I right? The 'ample food, comfortable bedrooms and good
off-duty times' mentioned in the letter above are pretty
wonderful and a fair sign that many of the adorable slatterns
we are married to have a notion (in their heads, probably)
that the Feudal System is still in operation. I have a fair
suspicion that 'ample food' is a misprint for *apple fool*, that
hideous mess of overboiled swede turnip and gooseberry
juice which the Nazis gleefully made the staple diet in French
concentration camps (Pièce de Résistance they called it, I
think!).

Imagine any lady *mentioning* the fact that the bare neces-
sities are accorded to her frail female help!!! Comfortable
bedrooms, by gor! Fwere in Eire are them pleasure domes to
be found? I am a fairly comfortable middle-aged man; I have
all my life been domiciled in this country: comfortable bedroom not once in that time have these mine eyes beheld, nor
have I the hearsay of the whereabouts of a divil a wan. (Of
course 'comfortable bedroom' might mean bedroom in which
only two of the walls are constantly damp, there's *that* to it.)
And the good 'off-duty times'—as though any time spent

away from that class of domestic enterprise could be anything but good! There was more:

The Housewives Association would do well to concern themselves with the employers' problems of the present time, instead of pandering to the already spoilt and indifferent domestic 'worker'.

There is no mention here of the nature of the employers' real problem—which is that their wives are too lazy to do housework and that they are consequently forced to hand out enormous sums every month for the maintenance of 'staff', which sums, the husbands well know, not more than ten per cent of into the pockets of the sairvint gairrls do go!

The same husbands have one other problem: namely, to figure out how it comes that they, who have chronic gastric and respiratory diseases from awful food and damp beds, apparently live in the same house as maids who have good food and comfortable beds! (I know the answer—or half of it—in my own case: *my* maid goes out to lunch!)

Two Stories

Here then is a story, written by Mee, famed associate of Tree, both noted for an exclusive attitude in regard to sitting under the apple.

A deep-sea diver, exploring the situation of a torpedoed man-of-war, was about to come to the surface when he noticed a young octopus in trouble. This not unhandy citizen —denizen of what but the deep?—had managed to get one of his 'feet' caught in the wreck, and was writhing in great agony. The diver, a kind-hearted man—albeit one crossed in love—decided to go to the succour of his fellow sub-acquate. Seizing a piece of steel wreckage, he prized away one of the baulks imprisoning the octopus's tentacle and thus released the unhappy sufferer.

The diver then, rejoicing in a good deed well done, turned to the ladder and gave his mate on the surface the signal to hoist. To his surprise, however, the young octopus began to accompany him upwards, paddling with great respect beside him. The look of gratitude on the large face of the octopus much moved the diver. Nevertheless, he made a deprecatory gesture and pushed the octopus away.

'Please go home,' he said.

'But sir,' the octopus cried, 'you have been so kind, so considerate, so helpful—I crave from you only the boon of accompanying you to your home, there to dwell with you for aye . . .!'

'Don't be a sucker,' the diver growled, 'where *I* live I haven't room for myself. You'll have to stay here in the sea. Anyway, I don't like that fancy inflated talk.'

'Kind sir,' the octopus implored, 'I will gladly live in your garden, or up a tree, or sit at night on the roof of your house. I will take up no room at all, sir. In the morning I will clean your boots. I will take the seaweed out of your diving boots. As well as that I will polish the floors. I have eight hands, you might say, sir, and would be very useful about the house and the yard.'

'Oh, don't be trying to *plamás* me,' the diver muttered.

'And I can go down into the sea with you,' the octopus besought.

'And get yourself caught in wreckage?'

'No sir, never again will I suffer that to occur. I will be most careful, sir. I will do anything you say if you permit me to live with you and repay your kindness.'

'Oh . . . very well,' the diver snapped. 'Swim over to that ship where you won't be seen coming out of the sea and I'll collect you in my van in an hour's time.'

'Oh, *thank* you, sir,' the octopus said, making what seemed to be a smile.

In due course the diver collected the octopus in his van, brought him home and lodged him in the dustbin until the following day, when he would have an opportunity of assigning him simple household tasks, so that his *bona fides* could be tested.

The octopus proved to be even better than his word. He proved expert at scrubbing and polishing floors, cleaned windows, made beds, lit fires and even learnt to make tea. He also managed to dig the garden after a fashion and never asked for a day off from his manifold duties.

After a year the diver had to admit that the octopus was a dear friend, and felt that some little token of esteem was called for. He therefore said to him one day:

'In another week it will be exactly a year since you came to this house. I feel I would like to give you a present to mark the occasion. Would you please tell me what you would like?'

The octopus blushed with pleasure.

'It is so terribly handsome of you,' he said, 'it is more than kind. And to answer your question, there is only one thing I would really like.'

'And what is that?'

'A bagpipes, sir.'

'A bagpipes it shall be,' the diver said, 'and the best that money can buy.'

On the day appointed the octopus was presented with his bagpipes. With cries of delight, he ran up with it to the attic where he customarily lodged. And after an interval the diver was horrified to hear blood-curdling screams, squeaks, roars,

wails and general din descending from the octopus's quarters.
What . . . on earth?

Rushing up to investigate, he was startled to find the bagpipes playing the octopus!

The Grandfather's Cousin

Did I ever tell you at all about the grandfather's mad cousin
that come home in the jigs every now and again from the
British Army?

He was sitting one day in a certain 'house' in the town of
Cavan, some distance from where he lived, which was
BALLYHAUNIS.

He asked the waitress for a glass of cold rain.

No misprint. That's what he asked for, to the astonish-
ment and puzzlement of the waitress. (The weather at the
time was unexceptionable.)

More betoken, the manager had to be sent for at the heel
of the hunt. After lengthy and skilful questioning, the
manager found that what my ancestor required was 'a glass
of Coleraine'—grand whiskey not made now.

When told that there was none 'in the place', he ordered a
taxi to go to Belfast and toured that city looking for a drop of
Coleraine with no result. (Even MacEntee's brother had
nothing only Power and Paddy.)

More betoken our friend hearing that there was 'bags' of
Coleraine in London, jumped the boat the same night and
arrived in that small hotel in Shaftesbury Avenue, not a
thousand miles from Wardour Street. (You know the place?)

In any case (and it was a normal case) he found a dozen
bottles of Coleraine there, drank four, and rang for a taxi to
bring him home.

When the taxi arrived at Liverpool, the client was un-
rousably asleep, so it was hoisted aboard, occupied, and the
driver went to the ship's bar to drink a bottle of ale and muse
on the nature of the mad Irish.

When taxi arrived at Dublin's North Wall, complete with
drunken passenger and puzzled driver, a Customs and Excise

man (who recognised the taxi's inmate) told the driver to make for Ballyhaunis.

Just outside Ballyhaunis the passenger awoke, surveyed the scenery suspiciously, and then told the driver to pull up. And the following talk took place:

'Stop here. What do I owe you?'

'Sixty-five pounds, sir.'

'Right.' (Produces wads of fivers, but keeps looking anxiously into the distance.) 'Is there any class of a town down there at all?'

'I think so, sir.'

'Thanks.' (Pays over seventy pounds. Gazes grimly into the distance.) 'I don't want you to go any further. If the crowd below seen me comin' home in a London taxi-cab, they might think I was drinking.'

And exit virtuously into the dark.

The John F. Byrne Irish Literature Series is made possible through a generous contribution by an anonymous individual. This contribution will allow Dalkey Archive Press to publish one book per year in this series.

Born and raised in Chicago, John F. Byrne was an educator and critic who helped to found the *Review of Contemporary Fiction* and was also an editor for Dalkey Archive Press. Although his primary interest was Victorian literature, he spent much of his career teaching modern literature, especially such Irish writers as James Joyce, Samuel Beckett, and Flann O'Brien. He died in 1998, but his influence on both the *Review* and Dalkey Archive Press will be lasting.